"I'm thankful for Rick Harrington, who passionately loves the church. And I'm thankful for his book *Churching*, which makes a case for the centrality of the church in God's plans. Read this book to rediscover the beauty and blessing of life in Christian community. Read it to rekindle your own love for the church, or to grow in helping others come back. Followers of Jesus are called to care about what he cares about—and Jesus loves his church."

—Stephen Witmer, co-founder, Small Town Summits

"We live in an odd and often unintelligible time when it comes to the issue of the local church. To hear professing Christians say that they love Jesus but hate his bride is a reflection of their ignorance of what Jesus himself said about the church. The simple and undeniable fact is that there is no such thing as a 'churchless' Christian. To what can we attribute this appalling approach to the local church? Many would point to pastoral bullying, clergy sexual abuse, the so-called 'prosperity' gospel, or perhaps the hypocrisy that so frequently abounds in the many gatherings of Christians. But there is no excuse for a Christian to turn his or her back on the bride of Christ. What the church is and does for the glory of God and the good of the believer is beautifully and biblically described in Rick Harrington's excellent book, *Churching*. If you've been hurt by the church or are tempted to abandon it, please read Rick's book. It is refreshing, convicting, and above all else, biblically true. It has my highest recommendation."

—Sam Storms, founder and president, Enjoying God Ministries

"It is impossible to read the New Testament without recognizing the vital role of the local church in the Christian life. Times have changed, but the nature of our calling remains the same. We were saved and called to belong to a spiritual family where our gifts, victories, and struggles come together to form a beautiful tapestry that reflects the true heart of the Father. *Churching* is a powerful and much-needed message for times like these. Let us embody the church way, for it is within this family that we can live out and experience all the promises of God—both for us and through us!"

—Carlito Paes, senior pastor, Church of the City, São José dos Campos, São Paulo, Brazil

"*Churching* masterfully weaves biblical ecclesiology with pastoral experience to address the critical challenge of dechurching in modern America. Through careful examination of ecclesia, koinonia, and the centrality of Christ's bride, he builds a compelling case for local church engagement that transcends individualistic Christianity. Drawing from his pastoral ministry in New England, where empty churches echo decline, Rick Harrington offers both theological depth and practical wisdom for rebuilding authentic church community."

—Gary J. Moritz, subject matter expert of church revitalization and renewal, Liberty University

"This is a challenging book and needs to be read. Rediscover what the church is: a spiritual family centered on an unchanging gospel of truth and the love of God. It is written out of pastoral experience and pastoral journeys."

—Paul Kim, founding pastor, Antioch Baptist Church in Cambridge, Massachusetts

CHURCHING

Churching

Rediscovering the
Centrality of the Church
in the Christian Life

RICK HARRINGTON

WIPF & STOCK · Eugene, Oregon

CHURCHING
Rediscovering the Centrality of the Church in the Christian Life

Copyright © 2025 Rick Harrington. All rights reserved. Except for brief quotations in critical publications or reviews, no part of this book may be reproduced in any manner without prior written permission from the publisher. Write: Permissions, Wipf and Stock Publishers, 199 W. 8th Ave., Suite 3, Eugene, OR 97401.

Wipf & Stock
An Imprint of Wipf and Stock Publishers
199 W. 8th Ave., Suite 3
Eugene, OR 97401

www.wipfandstock.com

PAPERBACK ISBN: 979-8-3852-3270-3
HARDCOVER ISBN: 979-8-3852-3271-0
EBOOK ISBN: 979-8-3852-3272-7

Scripture quotations are from The ESV® Bible (The Holy Bible, English Standard Version®), © 2001 by Crossway, a publishing ministry of Good News Publishers. Used by permission. All rights reserved.

To my local church, and local churches across the globe.

Contents

Acknowledgments xi

Introduction xiii

1 The Church Local 1

2 The Church of Christ 12

3 Communion of Saints 21

4 Authority Helps 33

5 Ordinary Ministry 42

6 Join the Party 55

7 The Church Is the Mission 68

8 The Good Rechurching 79

Conclusion 89

Bibliography 93

Acknowledgments

JUST AS IT TAKES a lifetime to write a sermon, meaning that every sermon comes from a lifetime of events experienced, books read, and conversations had, so it is true with drafting a book like this. Many pastor friends have had rich conversations with me over the topics covered in this book. My own church has heard me teach these issues over and again. My wife, Jessica, has been the perpetual sounding board for all my writing. Like the Lord's bride to Him, she is more valuable to me than anything in this world. Many, many thanks to all.

Introduction

THE DEAREST PLACE ON EARTH

WHAT IS *CHURCHING*? I define it as commitment and service to a local church. We have seen the rise of the term *dechurching* recently. Dechurching is the negation of churching, at least in the way I am using the word. It is the rejection of commitment and service to a local church. This is the way the groundbreaking book *The Great Dechurching*[1] uses the term. Dechurching is what has been happening in surprising numbers in the last 25 years. It is said that 40 million people have left the church in the United States alone. Though not recorded as carefully, dechurching started much earlier, as Ross Douthat noted, "Since the 1960s, the institutions that sustained orthodox Christian belief—Catholic and Protestant alike—have entered a state of near terminal decline."[2] The recent worldwide pandemic only made a downward trend worsen, "Covid-19, however, accelerated the long-trending separation between personal faith and organized religion."[3] Dechurching has been occurring throughout the lives of most Americans today. For those who grew up in the United States, it is all we have known.

The effects of the trend are all but inescapable, "No theological tradition, age group, ethnicity, political affiliation, education level,

---

1. Davis and Graham, *Great Dechurching*.
2. Douthat, *Bad Religion*, 3.
3. Hansen and Leeman, *Rediscover Church*, 11.

Introduction

geographic location, or income bracket escaped the dechurching in America."[4] Though no similar extensive study has been done, no doubt the situation in Europe is at least equally as severe. Even for those who attend a church, average weekly attendance is becoming less frequent, from once a week to a mere twice a month.[5] Whether you have been using the word *dechurching* or not, if you have been paying attention you have noticed churches closing, and those with commitment and service to a local church dwindling. We are losing the art of churching.

You might think that the verb form of church, *churching*, would have a long and well-known track record. Strangely enough, it does not. There is a historical use of the word, with a very niche meaning, dating back to the 15th century. The churching of women, as it was called, was the reintroduction of mothers and their babies after childbirth back to the church community. Beyond this, I found only a handful of uses of the word that defined the term similarly to the way I am using it, one being *The Churching of America* by historians Roger Finke and Rodney Stark,[6] and another as the title of a book translated from Russian to English.[7] I am hoping to employ an intuitive yet uncommon word and use it to encapsulate an old practice, a practice we desperately need to rediscover.

In this short book, I hope to persuade you, encourage you, even entice you to consider churching. There is a strong likelihood that you are a churchgoing Christian already. Serious Christians are the most likely to read Christian books, and most serious Christians are committed to a local church. I do not mean that as a slight on the dechurched, but merely as an observation. If you are reading this book as such a person, this book is for you. After all, the choir needs preaching to as much as anyone. If this book does nothing more than equip and encourage you who are already churching to endure in your commitment, and motivates you to

---

4. Davis and Graham, *Great Dechurching*, xxiii.
5. Rainer, "Decline in Church Attendance."
6. Finke and Stark, *Churching of America 1776–2005*.
7. Torik, *Churching*.

INTRODUCTION

invite those who are not to join you, it will have been a successful endeavor.

Maybe you are among the 40 million who have dechurched in the last 25 years, and part of you wants to try churching again. Surveys reveal that most who left are open to returning. It could be you are a new Christian trying to figure out the Christian life, and how the church fits in. Someone told you that you don't need a church, but you're rightly skeptical. Perhaps you are a churchgoer, but your attendance has been sporadic at best, and you need to know why church should matter to you at all. Are you not a Christian, but want to read a book to understand what church life is about? If so, this book is also for you.

I hope this book helps you understand the call upon the Christian to commit and serve the church. I want to muster an argument biblically, historically, and practically on behalf of the church. The church does not sit on the periphery of the Christian life; it belongs smack dab in the center. It is our means of grace to corporate worship, Christian fellowship, and the Great Commission. Like the churching of women, I want to introduce you and hopefully the next generation along the way to the church with fresh eyes.

I'm a pastor, not an academic. My hope is that you the reader might be encouraged to apply this book in your own life. The book is short by intention. I hope you read it through. Each of the eight chapters includes a section called *Wise Counsel*. Here I try to offer some practical advice on how to apply the content of the chapter. This is the kind of advice I have received, have given, or have heard given to others by wise Christian leaders. It may be helpful for you personally, or for how you counsel other people. Each chapter also includes discussion questions at the end. These are for your own reflection, or if you are reading the book with a friend or group they might foster some meaningful conversation between you.

The book is in no way exhaustive of all that can be included about what churching means. More could be said for example about church governance, spiritual warfare, or the spiritual gifts.[8]

---

8. For a theologically robust and practical defense of the charismatic

Introduction

I would rather whet your appetite and let your own study and church experience complete the meal. After all, the hope of the book is that the church becomes central to your Christian life.

I hope after reading the book you will agree that the church is not only a great blessing, but even with all its imperfections (including the ones we bring to it), a gift we should genuinely love. As the ever-quotable C. H. Spurgeon once claimed:

> In the next place, follow this example, and give yourself to the church. You that are members of the church have not found it perfect, and I hope that you feel almost glad that you have not. If I had never joined a church till I had found one that was perfect, I should never have joined one at all; and the moment I did join it, if I had found one, I should have spoiled it, for it would not have been a perfect church after I had become a member of it. Still, imperfect as it is, it is the dearest place on earth to us.[9]

---

spiritual gifts for the church today, consider reading Storms, *Practicing the Power*.

9. Spurgeon, *Metropolitan Pulpit Sermons*, 37:633.

1

The Church Local

WHAT IS ECCLESIA?

I HAD ARRIVED IN Nepal less than twenty-four hours before. That was an experience. Coming off the plane, the third-world airport was packed with jostling people speaking a language I could not understand. Hustlers were eager to take advantage of foreigners, quickly carrying my bags without asking and then demanding a tip. Thoughts entered my mind about whether I had just made a serious mistake traveling halfway around the world to the foothills of the Himalayas. I felt like a speck that would get lost in this ocean of people and never be found again. This all changed when I met Titus and Benjamin.[1] The moment I met these Christian Nepalis a switch flipped in my heart. We hugged and chatted, then laughed and told stories, without fully understanding one another. It was as if we were back in New England hanging out on my own porch.

Back to twenty-four hours after arrival, however. I was sleep deprived and jet lagged, energized only by adrenaline. I had been invited to preach in Kathmandu, Nepal's capital city. We met in the shadow of a large Hindu temple a mere block away. The meeting space was about the size of a large storage unit and looked like one, as I recall. The room was stuffed with people, no AC, and little

---

1. It is typical for Nepali Christians to choose biblical names so that their English-speaking friends can more easily remember them.

ventilation. There were no seats, except the plastic lawn chairs in the very back row where they allowed their honored guests to sit. Everyone else sat crisscrossed on the floor. The worship was loud and lively; even the teenagers were swaying. (I did however see the pastor smack one of them in the back of the head for goofing off!) The prayers were vibrant, even if I could not understand them.

I preached on the parable of the prodigal son, from Luke 15:11–32, through a translator. To my surprise, two young women responded to the pastor's call to trust in Jesus Christ. It certainly was not due to my rhetorical flourish! I later asked my guide what would happen next for the girls. He said the pastor would meet with them and require them to dispose of all other "gods" in their home. He will then begin to disciple them. After the service, we met with the pastor and his family at his home for lunch. I ate some fruit that I didn't even know existed until then.

Churches Are Us

You are not the church. I realize this statement goes against the modern spirit of Christianity in much of the Western world. Church signs, banners, and coffee mugs proliferate with the slogan "You are the church."[2] Yet, it is a saying that would puzzle most Christians throughout church history—certainly the first-century followers of The Way (see Acts 9:2; 19:9, 12; 24:14, 22).

The Greek word behind the English "church" is *ecclesia*. Its essential meaning is an assembly. As the definitive lexicon of the Greek New Testament translates it, an "assembly, gathering, or congregation."[3] The word *ecclesia* had a preexistent meaning before it was applied to the early Christians, though. The term "was in common usage for several hundred years before the Christian era and was used to refer to an assembly of persons constituted by

---

2. If "you" (plural) is meant, then the phrase could be used in a meaningful sense when spoken to a congregation. However, it is often used to speak to individuals, as in "you (singular) are the church," which is what this chapter is addressing. The very ambiguity of the phrase is part of the problem with it.

3. Bauer et al., *Greek-English Lexicon*, s.v. "ecclesia."

well-defined membership."[4] What we might call civic or work conferences today would have no problem identifying their gathering as *ecclesia*. The word is used in the New Testament to describe such gatherings (see Acts 19:32; 39–40).

This is not to say there was no Scriptural precedent for using *ecclesia* to refer to Christian assemblies. In the Septuagint, the Greek translation of the Old Testament, it was used to refer to the assembly of Israel (e.g., Deut 4:10; Judg 20:2; Esd 10:1). The gathering of the people of God in ancient Israel gave the New Testament writers the perfect word to describe Christians as they gathered throughout the Roman Empire.

Theologians often speak of the church universal. This is a description of all Christians throughout the world and sometimes including those already in glory (that is, the church triumphant). The church universal, as opposed to the church local, will one day gather as one united entity at the end of history, with representatives from every tongue, tribe, and nation.

> After this I looked, and behold, a great multitude that no one could number, from every nation, from all tribes and peoples and languages, standing before the throne and before the Lamb, clothed in white robes, with palm branches in their hands, and crying out with a loud voice, "Salvation belongs to our God who sits on the throne, and to the Lamb!" (Rev 7:9–10)

What a sight that will be! Every genuine believer will be there, and every church-going hypocrite excluded. The bride of Christ will together enjoy the wedding feast of the Lamb. It will be an assembly like never imagined in all of human history. Come, Lord Jesus! I digress.

From what you hear from today's chatter, one would think the church universal is the primary use of *ecclesia* in the New Testament and every so often a reference is made to the local get-together. The truth is the exact opposite. While we await that glorious end-time multitude, our primary *ecclesia* today is a local gathering. This is incontestably the majority use of the word

---

4. Louw and Nida, *Greek-English Lexicon*, s.v. "ecclesia," 125.

in the Greek New Testament. *Ecclesia* is primarily used not as an eschatological (end-times) entity, but as an actual gathering of Christian believers in a particular geographical locale. Whether a church is in Jerusalem or Rome, Corinth or Crete, Antioch or Athens, Christians gathered with God's people locally.

No one individual can say, "I am the church," as the very word connotes an assembly. I can say I am part of a church. Even better, I can say, along with a church family on Sunday morning, "*We* are the church." You and I, individually, are not the church nor should we want to be. We need others. I am a believer, a follower of Jesus Christ, a child of God, even, but church is something I cannot be without my fellow Christians.

One You Can Kiss and Smell

Every Sunday morning, Sandra, our greeter, gives me a big hug and a kiss on the cheek (we suggested she not kiss newcomers). When I step into our cafe, I smell the fresh baked desserts that Debbie made for early arrivers. Gary will already be there, having unlocked the doors and put out the church signs. I can hear the praise team rehearsing in the background. It would not be unusual for some glitch to come up that needs addressing: a sound system issue or lack of toilet paper in the restroom.

Eventually, I will head into the sanctuary and see familiar faces who smile and chat. We will start to sing together and pray together. I know who sings softly and who sings loudly (and who sings off key). I know who is likely to laugh at my attempt at sermon humor and who will more likely roll their eyes. I even know those who will get up to use the restroom during the worship service . . . and when!

I also know that John is battling cancer and hopeful of a liver transplant. Roberta struggles with Sjorgren's disease. David's granddaughter has Transverse Myelitis. I know Jim's Huntington's disease is progressing. I know the newlyweds, those who have recovered from addiction, and one who recently received custody of his child. I realize you do not know these people. The point is,

I do. Church is not an ethereal entity; it is a tangible assembly. As Christians, the church is not merely a theological concept. It is also a very real gathering of the saints.

COVID-19 did the American church a favor. As horrible as it was for so many people, especially those who lost loved ones, it did the church an invaluable service. It reminded us that we cannot replace actual gatherings with Zoom meetings or Facebook Live. Not even close. The prognosticators got it wrong. The replacement of church with online services was entirely insufficient. It started to die off before COVID did. Even for introverts who enjoyed the comfort of tuning in from the privacy of our own homes, we could all see what was blatantly obvious: this is not church. There is something indispensable about looking a brother in the eye when he talks with you about his week or hugging a sister who is hurting with financial stress or laughing together when some small quirk goes haywire during gathered worship. *We* are the church.

The Church's Home

I love old church buildings. There is nothing wrong with Christians meeting in a warehouse, a school, or even a shopping mall. The gathering is not limited to any architectural structure or barred from enjoying the open air. The church in Jerusalem met in the temple before it was destroyed in AD 70. In Ephesus, they used a lecture hall owned by a man named Tyrant (Gr. Tyrannus; see Acts 19:9)! Mostly they met in homes belonging to members of the congregation. Churches did not even have designated buildings until the third century.[5]

The church is not a building. For some reading this, they may still associate a church with a particular structure in town. If my historic sanctuary built in 1882 burned down today, my church would weep, but that weeping church would still exist. That sanctuary, after all, is the church's fourth building, not including the

---

5. The earliest known building designated exclusively for use by a church is the Dura Europos in Syria. This home, in which two rooms were combined to form an assembly room, was converted into church usage in the 240s.

home of John Duncan in 1765. My church is composed of the members who assemble in Haverhill, Massachusetts, as First Baptist Church.

A church facility is to a church what a house is to a home. It is where all the family most often meets, and it is where you invite guests to join you. If you need to expand, you add an addition. If you need to downgrade, you put up a for sale sign. You do your best to take care of it, leaky roof, creaky doors, and all, because it says something about how well you value your place in the community. Your family, however, is something far more valuable than brick and mortar.

Personally, I love a good old chapel, a facility dedicated to no other purpose than the worship of God. Give me a tall white steeple pointing the city towards the heavens and a high wood pulpit placed front and center for the proclamation of the word of God. My New England heritage is showing. Many meeting houses in New England date back to the seventeenth and eighteenth century, built during the end of the Puritan era. The remains of George Whitefield, the great evangelist of the First Great Awakening, lie under the Old South Presbyterian Church in Newburyport, Massachusetts, a few miles away from where I live. You can visit the church building and get a tour, ending with a viewing of his crypt with a mold of his skull!

Before I start to sound too nostalgic, I will admit this: the building is just a tool. It is an expensive tool. It is the largest tool a church possesses—for some, the size of a Super Walmart, though for others, more like a double-wide trailer. It is most often a useful tool. Yet at the end of the day, that is all it is. It is a tool for the congregation to congregate.

The Size of the Assembly

The Bible is not anti-megachurch. The church in Jerusalem numbered in the multiple thousands. The assembly in Philemon's house was probably no more than a few dozen. The New Testament does not prescribe any ideal size, nor does it place any limits on how big or how small a church must be. Church sizes are meant to vary, displaying something about the diversity of the kingdom. Regaining an appreciation for small churches (while not demonizing large churches) has been a move towards Christian unity and maturity, as Stephen Witmer, cofounder of Small Town Summits writes,

> There will be some facets of God's character and God's gospel that my small church in my small town simply can't display as well as a three-thousand member church in a great city. But the opposite will be true as well. Some precious facets of the gospel will be seen more clearly in a small church in a small place than anywhere else.[6]

Location makes a difference. Here in New England, small towns make up the bulk of churches; where any church over one hundred members outside of Boston is a big church!

It is not surprising that churches in general are getting smaller, as dechurching continues. We are a long way from declaring time of death on the megachurch, but the trend is toward smaller, community churches. This trend could change tomorrow, and we would be no better or worse necessarily. What matters is whether the size of the church is conducive to people being well-shepherded and having access to genuine fellowship. More on this later.

The Church Scattered

Though the essential nature of *ecclesia* is never lost (Christians who come together), *ecclesia* is used derivatively of the people scattered from the assembly and going about their lives. The church is the church when gathered and remains the church when scattered. To scatter, you must first gather. The church in Corinth or Troas met weekly, on the first day of the week. Then the church went back to their day jobs and spread the gospel through the city. If they stopped gathering altogether, soon the very essence of the church

---

6. Witmer, *Big Gospel*, 74.

would be in jeopardy. Within a few years, it would cease to exist entirely.

The New England Patriots dominated throughout my kids' childhoods. We have had a chance to meet a few players over the years. At one event, we got to meet Matthew Slater, future Hall of Famer and special teams captain (he is also a devout Christian). Slater was a New England Patriot, even when he was signing his autograph to a football after giving a talk at Gordon-Conwell Theological Seminary. However, if the New England Patriots had gone out of business and stopped meeting as a team, he would no longer have been a New England Patriot (he would still of course forever be a former Patriot). If the team ceased to be, the players are no longer representatives of that team. The same can be said of a church and its members.

What of those who cannot make the assembly due to health concerns or particular vocations? They remain part of the church scattered for a time. The exceptions confirm the rule. For our shut-ins, as a church, we recognize that these members are in a hard situation. They would gather with us if they could. I have had members sit through services in severe pain whom I could not convince to stay home if I tried (sweet Lottie is resting in peace with her Savior now). Others know they cannot make it. Many will not gather with us again until we all get together in glory. We love them. We miss them. We don't abandon a man down.

Certainly, Christians should do our best to agree to not work when the church gathers. Yet even the Puritans understood there are certain necessary Sabbath-time vocations.[7] For our doctors and nurses, police officers and emergency responders, working on Sunday mornings, we understand. We see you. The gathering is not a chain around our necks; it is a blessing to which we are eager to return. Exceptions like this do not disprove the rule; they highlight its importance.

---

7. For example, the Synod of Dort, in discussing rest from Sabbath work, mentions "with these excepted, which are works of charity and pressing necessity." Synod of Dort, quoted in Ligonier, "Sabbath," para. 9.

All the church scatters. No one congregates all day, every day. Every church-going Christian will spend most of his or her time as the church scattered. This is the time we go about our lives living out our faith in the home and the marketplace. We act as ambassadors in a country not our own. We are witnesses as we anticipate the next gathering. Our assembly is the fountain out of which all our scattering out into the world flows.

A Grotesque Anomaly

The late John Stott famously stated, "I trust that none of my readers is that grotesque anomaly, an un-churched Christian. The New Testament knows nothing of such a person. For the church lies at the very center of the eternal purpose of God."[8] It would be hard to overemphasize the importance of the local church. Yet, the Christian life without commitment to a church is becoming the new norm.

America is dechurching. In the past twenty-five years, approximately forty million people have left their churches. This is not merely people walking away from the faith. Many *Christians* have dechurched as well. Many who still hold to orthodox Christian doctrine no longer associate with any church.[9] They vigorously defend their rejection of the church as a spiritual improvement. They see membership as an optional club, and the gathering as a sort of side issue in the real business of following Jesus. They believe they have leveled up.

Let me ask a basic question: Is Christianity in the United States spiritually healthier today than it was twenty-five years ago? Is this jettison of *ecclesia* a sign of spiritual health or decline? Let me make it more personal. Are the Christians you know

---

8. Stott, *Living Church*, 20.

9. Speaking of "ex-vangelicals" in particular, "Overall they affirmed between 70 percent of key doctrinal questions concerning the Trinity, the divinity/humanity of Jesus, his sinlessness, atonement, resurrection, and exclusivity, and the reliability of the Bible. A surprising 97 percent of them still believe that 'Jesus is the Son of God.'" See Davis and Graham, *Great Dechurching*, 71.

who walked away from a local church more vibrant now in their faith than they were when actively participating and serving in a church? Are they more loving, self-sacrificial, and empathetic to others than they once were? I cannot speak for everyone, but most of the ones I know have a chip on their shoulder they are eager to moan about, or more likely post on social media about. I agree with Collin Hansen and Jonathan Leeman's warning: "A Christian without a church is a Christian in trouble."[10]

Even if you disagree, and you believe that Christians are happier and healthier after detangling themselves from the church, such individualism has led to bad religion, a theological worldview estranged from historic orthodox Christianity. As Roth Douthat writes,

> The United States remains a deeply religious country, and most Americans are still drawing some water from the Christian well. But a growing number are inventing their own versions of what Christianity means, abandoning the nuances of traditional theology in favor of religions that stroke their ego and indulge or even celebrate their worst impulses.[11]

Bad theology exists in churches too, but the individualism that dechurching fosters leads to a "me first" approach to Christianity. What, after all, is dechurching but deciding to separate from the community and go it alone?

Some might argue a chicken-and-egg scenario here: it is the spiritual unhealthiness of the church that caused the dechurching, not dechurching that led to spiritual unhealthiness. I have no intent to defend the church as innocent and put all the blame on the individuals who left. There is more than enough guilt to go around. This moment cries out for reevaluation. This book will do a lot of self-examination for the church, I hope. What I do know is that leaving the church behind has not produced spiritual healthiness among Christians. Nor do I believe that churching is the only factor towards spiritual vitality, but I know it is part of the equation.

10. Hansen and Leeman, *Rediscover Church*, 11.
11. Douthat, *Bad Religion*, 4.

Let's have the church do better, and let's encourage the dechurched to come back.

Wise Counsel

Find a church. Take your time and do your research but be sure to gather with a local church and take steps to be part of it. Congregate with them regularly on Sundays (or whatever day they meet corporately). Get up, throw on some clothes, and head out the door, even when you don't feel like it. If need be, sneak in late and sit in the back row or the balcony for the time being. Say hello to the pew warmers sitting around you and use that time to pray and listen to the Lord.

Discussion Questions

1. Describe your own church background. Do you have a positive or negative view of the local church now? How has your commitment to a local church changed over the years? If you have dechurched, do you still believe Jesus is Savior and Lord?

2. Why is it important that no *one* person can call themselves a church? Why do you think online services did not replace church attendance for most people, as many expected? What is it about physical presence with other Christian believers that is invaluable?

3. When the church scatters, do you look forward to meeting again? What would happen to your church if it stopped meeting together entirely? How does your church care for those who can no longer gather due to health or vocation?

4. Have you ever been to church in countries outside of the United States? What was similar across cultures? What was different? What do you think Americans can learn from how other cultures experience church?

2

The Church of Christ

UPON THIS ROCK

I DIDN'T REALLY KNOW what I was doing when I started youth ministry. I certainly had no business being called a youth *pastor*. We played crazy and dangerous games that sometimes physically hurt. I distinctly remember one trust fall game when I asked the kids to fall backwards from the sanctuary stage down to the rest of us standing ready to catch them. Johnny bravely took the initiative and stepped up to the platform, turned around, and closed his eyes. He fell backwards and . . . *we missed the catch*. His initiative and courage were rewarded with bruises. Not the message I was hoping to convey. He likely never regained his confidence in our ability to have his back.

A few months later, I figured, since we are a youth group, we should go on a youth retreat. I did not want to do the typical New England strategy and take the teens to the backwoods of New Hampshire for some quiet reflection. I was too cool for that, or so I thought. Instead, I planned a trip for about twenty teenagers to go to New York City. That would be the perfect setting to talk about community.

While in the Big Apple, I decided we would tour the United Nations. We could see diverse community in action! I did nothing to prepare the teens for our visit. Most of them were not even sure what the United Nations was. When a tour guide asked if anyone in the group knew who a picture of the secretary general was (Kofi Annan, at the time), one teen answered, in all seriousness, "Bill Cosby?"

One aspect of Manhattan I did not consider carefully enough (there were a lot of them) was transportation. How do we get a group of twenty teens safely around the city? Safely is a word I use lightly. We taxied teens who were not really supposed to ride without an adult from place to place. We took the subway and almost started a fight. At one point, we walked through Central Park at night. Two of the more distracted kids kept separating from the pack. One adult volunteer quipped, "This is normally where natural selection thins the herd." Thankfully, we all returned with nothing but slight psychological scars.

The one thing I think I did particularly well in youth ministry, and what the teenagers would remember most about our time (besides the trip), was to constantly reinforce the vision: "Jesus-centered community." Our goal as a youth group was to be a community based on Jesus. That, I told them, is what the youth group, as a ministry of our local church, is all about. Jesus must be the center of our fellowship.

Jesus Versus the Church?

There is a rumor going around that Jesus does not much like the church. He is sort of annoyed with his bride, if not outright disgusted by her. Some might even suggest a breakup. This animosity has led people to the conclusion that they can love Jesus and hate the church. See if these statements sound familiar:

"I believe in Jesus, but I don't go to church."

"I have no problem with Jesus, but I don't do organized religion."

"Jesus was about personal faith not *churchianity*."

Being a devoted part of a local church has almost become a sign of spiritual immaturity for our day; if you were serious about Jesus, you would not be able to put up with church people. We have even come up with that new curse word, *churchianity*. The idea is Christianity was about Christ, but churchianity has tainted it with the church.

Does this divorce between Jesus and the church hold up to what Jesus himself taught? Did the early Christians take Jesus's teachings and run off to create some organized religion that he never wanted? It is important to let Jesus speak for himself on this topic.

Jesus's Use of Ecclesia

Before the Christian church even existed, Jesus spoke about it. He used the word *ecclesia* specifically in two contexts: Matt 16 and 18. Before we examine these, it is valuable to grasp how significant this is. He was speaking of a reality yet to be. Rather than scoffing that he only referred to ecclesia twice, we should be surprised that he mentions ecclesia at all. This has even caused some more liberal scholars to question whether these were later interpolations.

Matthew 16:13–20 is particularly poignant. At a key moment in his ministry, Jesus asked his disciples who people say he is. Some say a prophet, others Elijah, and still others John the Baptist back from the dead. Jesus turned the question on the disciples themselves: Who do you say I am? Simon Peter had a remarkable moment of clarity: I say you are the Christ, the Son of the living God. Jesus commended him that this insight was revealed by none other than God the Father. Lest Simon Peter get too big of a head, it was not long after that Jesus rebuked him, "Get behind me, Satan" (16:23). That is quite a drastic fall.

Jesus changed Simon's name to Peter and told him, upon this rock, he will build his ecclesia. He qualifies the ecclesia as that against which the gates of Hades will not prevail. The church will advance throughout the world breaking down hell's gates everywhere it goes, freeing its captives. Jesus gave the keys of the kingdom to bind and loose on earth what had been bound or loosed in heaven. It was undoubtedly a climactic moment in the ministry of Jesus, one in which he revealed the whole purpose of his life, death, and resurrection as for the church!

The second ecclesia passage is Matt 18:15–20. Less climatic but equally important, this pericope of teaching is where Jesus spelled out the responsibility of the church's binding and loosing. If a brother sins against you, go show him his fault just between the two of you. If there is no repentance, bring witnesses (who might conversely clarify that the accuser is mistaken). If there is still no repentance, bring it to the ecclesia. The church then acts as heaven's emissary. If there is no repentance still, the church is to treat him as a gentile or tax collector, not meaning to hate the sinner but rather not recognize him as part of the kingdom. Eternity will tell, but the church offers no stamp of validation. Assumedly, if there is true repentance, the church declares his forgiveness in Christ. What God has loosed, let no one bind.

This assumed a gathering. What would the ecclesia we report to be but a local congregation of Christians? How would the ecclesia assess the individual without an assembly of believers? It is in this context, we get the familiar promise, "Again I say to you, if two of you agree on earth about anything they ask, it will be done for them by my Father in heaven. For where two or three are gathered in my name, there am I among them" (Matt 18:19–20). This unique presence of God with his people is not in the setting of a backyard hangout or a seminary classroom but in the context of a church congregation.

Feed My Sheep

The approach thus far is too minimizing of Jesus's emphasis on the church. Simply examining when Jesus used the word ecclesia does not exhaust his teaching on the church. One could argue that his entire ministry was about the church: calling his disciples to be brothers, teaching them to love one another as servants, infusing the Passover with new eucharistic meaning, and commissioning his followers to baptize disciples. These were all ways to prepare them for what was to come.

After the resurrection, Jesus breaks Peter's heart. He asks him if he loves him more than the others. Peter quickly replies, "Yes." *Then feed my lambs.* He says a second time, "Do you love me?" "Yes." *Then tend my lambs.* Jesus inquired a third time, "Do you love me?" and with a grieved heart Peter answered again, "Lord you know all things, you know that I love you." Jesus answers yet a third time, *Feed my sheep* (see John 21:15-19). Many see this as a restoration, counteracting Peter's three denials of Jesus. Note how Jesus expects Peter to display his love for him by shepherding the flock of God (see 1 Pet 5:1–5). The ongoing ministry of the apostles will be to take care of the church.

Red and Black

Considering Jesus's words only, to the exclusion of the teaching of the apostles, is a bad *modus operandi*. Red letter Christianity is doomed to fail. Since some Bibles have the words of Jesus printed in red, some Christians have opted for a Christianity based on the red lettering exclusively, excluding the teachings of Paul, for example, as not relevant for us today.[1] As we have seen, there is more than enough in the teaching of Jesus to put the church back in the center of the Christian life. Yet the problems with this narrow approach to Christianity are manifold. Set aside that putting the words of Jesus in red lettering is a modern publishing convention, we are still left with insurmountable obstacles.

We do not have any of Jesus's writings. It is unlikely he wrote any of his own teaching down, save a few scribblings in the sand (John 8:6). Every word we know from Jesus comes to us through his apostles. If you do not trust their interpretation of Jesus's teaching, how can you trust that they faithfully transmitted his words? Before long, you will have to discount the red letters as an invention of the apostles just the same. Many, of course, have done just

---

1. There is even a Red Letter Christians movement started in 2007 and growing, founded by Tony Campolo and Shane Claiborne. See the Red Letter Christians website at https://redletterchristians.org/about-us/our-mission-our-story/.

that. The Gospel according to John seems to be a common target for more liberal scholars.

Some might argue, still, they trust the gospel writers more so than, say, 1 Corinthians or 1 Timothy. Paul was too worried about institutionalized Christianity; he lost all objectivity about Jesus's own teaching, they claim. This again misses the mark. Let alone that Luke was a close companion of Paul, still Matthew, Mark, and John wrote their Gospels for the church! They wanted the church strengthened by what they wrote. Yes, they sought to reliably transmit Jesus's teaching, but they wrote their accounts with an end in mind just the same. Out of the endless miracles and didactic material they could have included (see John 21:25), they chose what they did because they believed it would strengthen the body of Christ. That, many would suggest, is why we have four Gospel writers, each writing with a different emphasis for a different church audience.

Like it or not, it is all or nothing when it comes to the New Testament, or with both testaments for that matter. Jesus not only believed in the divine authority of the Old Testament, the New Testament teaches the Hebrew Scriptures were written by him (John 1:1) and about him (John 5:39–40). Written in red, Jesus said, "before Abraham was, I am" (John 8:58).

The Rest of the Story

Luke's biography of Jesus has a part two. The ministry of Jesus continued with the advance of the Christian church and the establishment of local churches throughout Jerusalem, Judea, Samaria, and the ends of the earth. Theophilus, Luke's recipient, surely got the picture that Acts was a continuation of what "Jesus began to do and teach" (Acts 1:1). One can hardly think of the life of Jesus without consequently considering the acts of the apostles following his resurrection.

In the book of Acts, Paul encouraged the Ephesian elders to "pay careful attention to yourselves and to all the flock, in which the Holy Spirit has made you overseers, to care for the church of

God, which he obtained with his own blood" (20:28). The interchangeable wording of "God" and Jesus Christ notwithstanding (it is Jesus who bled), the church is the entity Jesus obtained with his own death. The high calling of shepherding the church is exponentially inflated by the price Jesus would pay for his sheep.

Paul, formerly Saul, "persecuted the church of God" (1 Cor 15:9) until one day the resurrected Jesus appeared to him on the road to Damascus and declared, "Saul, Saul why are you persecuting me?"[2] (Acts 9:4). Paul never met the incarnate Jesus before this. He had no interactions with him that we know of. Yet, Jesus so identifies himself with his people that to persecute the church is to persecute Jesus himself. Some have argued that not only Paul's doctrine of grace but his doctrine of union with Christ can be traced back to his conversion. Jesus identifies himself with the church, and the church with himself.

As for the apostle Paul's epistles, he wrote no higher view of Jesus's love for the church than this: "And [God the Father] put all things under his feet and gave him as head over all things to the church, which is his body, the fullness of him who fills all in all" (Eph 1:22–23). Through the church he makes known to angels on high the manifold wisdom of God (3:10). Jesus is given as head over all *to the church*.[3]

The New Testament ends as it began in Matthew, with Jesus building his church. The book of Revelation is addressed to the seven churches: "John to the seven churches that are in Asia" (Rev 1:4). These are not Christian get-togethers but local church assemblies: Ephesus, Smyrna, Pergamum, Thyatira, Sardis, Philadelphia, and Laodicea. The revelation of Jesus is "to the angel of the church in" each of these cities. The seven churches are not merely the prelude to the Apocalypse, the entire book is written "for the churches" (Rev 22:16).

2. Saul was Paul's Hebrew name.

3. The phrase "to the church" is either a dative of advantage, meaning that Christ is given for the church (NIV, NRSV) or a dative of indirect object, in which case Christ is the gift given to the church (AV, NASB, ESV). While the second is more likely (given the word "give"), both would make the church central to the entire ministry of Jesus.

The Church of Christ

Jesus Loves His Bride

I love my wife. We have been married twenty-five years, and I still light up when I pick her up from work. It is safe to say that if you do not like my wife, we won't be friends. I won't hate you, but she is such a part of my life that I cannot imagine being close to someone who has no interest in her. To spurn her is to spurn me and vice versa. Of course, you are far more likely to like her than me, but that is beside my point. The church is the bride of Christ (Eph 5:32; Rev 19:7). He loves her. He adores her in all her current imperfections. He would never abandon her.

Alright, I'll ease up a little bit. The church can be a problem. Like Israel in the Old Testament, the Christian church can be a wayward wife. She loves her idols. She often yearns for worldly power and praise. Many people have been hurt deeply by a local church (more on this later in the book). To look at Jesus is to see *perfection*; to look at the church is to see *redemption*. Redemption has two sides—one as beautiful as a glimpse of heaven itself but the other, ugly as hell. Like Hosea's Gomer (see Hos 1–3), she is a work in progress, but she never ceases to be his bride.

There is no clear path to revival apart from Christ's bride. Christian bestsellers, robust seminary enrollment, and megaconferences won't get us there. The means of grace towards renewal runs through Jesus-centered community.

Wise Counsel

Ask Jesus to help you love the church. Read one of the four gospels with eyes wide open about what he is saying about the church and to the church. Skip ahead and read Ephesians. Highlight, circle, or underline every reference to the church. Then go back and read Acts. Look around your church and think about how you could serve to make it a better reflection of what Jesus intended for his bride.

CHURCHING

Discussion Questions

1. Why do you think people are drawn to a personal relationship with Jesus Christ but are sometimes repelled by his church? How is loving Jesus often much easier than loving the church?

2. What did Jesus himself teach us during his earthly ministry about the church? What responsibility did he give to his apostles when it came to caring for fellow believers? In the book of Revelation, how does Jesus teach the church to be faithful in hard times?

3. How does the image of the church as Jesus's bride demonstrate his love for the church? How would our love and commitment for the church be enhanced if we thought more often of the church as the bride of Christ?

4. What does the perceived animosity between Jesus and the church say about the current state of Christianity in the United States? How might a rekindled love of the church lead to spiritual renewal?

3

Communion of Saints

FELLOWSHIP MATTERS

I LOVE THE CHINESE people. By some estimates there are as many as one hundred million Christians throughout the People's Republic of China, many of whom meet below the radar in house churches. I was there with a group of "tourists," entering the Forbidden City, walking on the Great Wall, taking pictures of the Shanghai Tower, and admiring the terra-cotta warriors in Xi'an. This was pre-pandemic, so we could freely travel, and everything was open to the public. I even learned how to bargain for a chess set for my son (I still paid too much yuan). Along the way we had the opportunity to meet with house church pastors over savory Chinese dinners.[1] I told our guide that I am half Korean. From that point on, at dinner he made sure they brought out the extra spicy stuff for me!

To say these conversations with Chinese pastors were life changing would be an understatement. The insights offered were astonishing. Among the most stunning was one pastor's statement, "We pray that the Lord does not take away the persecution against

1. We also visited a couple of Three-Self Churches, the government-sanctioned Protestant churches in China. I was surprised at how biblically faithful the preaching was during these visits. With cameras watching the services, I was expecting carefully edited sermons, but that was not my anecdotal experience.

the Chinese church. Not yet. Eventually, yes, but we are not ready yet." In one conversation, the house church pastor mentioned in passing that he was arrested during a recent gathering. I asked him to revisit that and explain what happened. He said, "They do this to intimidate you. They bring you in on some false charge, interrogate you for a day, and then let you go."

I felt worlds apart from American Christianity. Churching in China meant risking your freedom, job, and reputation. In many parts of the world, it means risking your life. I can only imagine what one of these house church pastors would think of the American Christian who says, "I don't go to church because I need Sundays to catch up on my sleep" or "I stopped going to services after someone said something rude to me." Their puzzled look would be all we would need to see.

Acting like Family

I have argued that if churches cease to meet, in time they cease to exist. But what is it about meeting that makes it so special? What happens when Christians meet that makes assembling crucial to spiritual vitality? Why would people, like so many Chinese Christians, risk their freedom and livelihood for the privilege of getting together? We will get into specifics like baptism and the Lord's Table later, but for now let's just summarize the meetings as *fellowship*.

What characterizes the gathering together of the church is fellowship (Gr. *koinonia*). This is more than friendship. It is an expression of a divinely established unity the church has. To be clear, we do not create unity, nor do we break it. We have this unity from our union with Christ, and we enjoy it in the context of the church gathering in fellowship. You cannot break your spiritual unity with a fellow Christian, but you can break fellowship with her. Fellowship is something we choose to engage in, or not.

One of the most common ways to refer to other Christians in the Scriptures is as brothers and sisters. The family imagery is pervasive, from the way Jesus spoke of us (e.g., Matt 12:50) to the way the apostles addressed churches (e.g., Gal 1:2). Like a family, we are united. In one sense, we are united *like it or not*. Even if two siblings fight with each other, they are still family. They may constantly bicker, roll their eyes at each other, or even accidently kick the other's head into a wall (may have happened in my household). Worse yet, they may ignore each other and hardly see each other. Yet we all know that is not how brothers and sisters should act. A parent might even say, "Start acting like brothers!" We all know what she means.

The church is a spiritual family. The gathering is a time to act like spiritual siblings. I sometimes wonder if, just as marriage symbolizes the union of Jesus and the church (not the other way around), so likewise, our earthly families were created as the temporal symbol of the eternal reality of Christian brotherhood. Like a family, we live out of our God-given unity. We practice Christian fellowship. After all, we are going to be together for an eternity!

The Law of Conformity

We are influenced by our network of friends. This is one of the most important factors in figuring out what kind of character a person has, how successful he will be, and even how healthily she will live. Our grandmothers had it right: tell me who your friends are, and I will tell you who you are. The New Testament beat them to the punch: "Bad company corrupts good morals" (1 Cor 15:33), which may itself be a reference to the even older comedy *Thais* by Menander (ca. 300 BC).[2] Even if so, the book of Proverbs had the Greeks by a few more centuries: "Whoever walks with the wise becomes wise, but the companion of fools will suffer harm" (Prov 13:20). It not only takes a village to raise a child, but the village is also an inescapable mold the child will grow into. If he wants to change the mold, he needs to find a new village.

Like many people, I can remember my high school days to be times of some anxiety. When a particular social group didn't

---

2. Fee, *First Corinthians*, 773.

accept me, or when I got cut from a sports team, it felt like the world was going to end. Then I went to college. Just like that, my horizons opened to new vistas, and much of the anxiety of high school felt small by comparison. I chose a major and was surrounded by others pursuing similar goals in life. After college, I got married and moved to Chicago to begin seminary. College life appeared worlds apart in hindsight as my social world expanded to married couples dealing with home purchases and friends having babies and raising kids. Travelling internationally, I befriended people with vastly different lifestyles and beliefs. My perspective of life broadened even further. I didn't know what I didn't know. (I wonder how much I still don't know about the world!) As my network of friends changed and expanded, I changed along with it.

It is not that we are doomed to be like our community or even that we must forget about where we came from to grow (like most people, I keep in contact with some friends from high school and college, who have also grown). What we can do is intentionally decide the type of people with which we surround ourselves and how much time we spend around them. We can consciously choose the people we allow to influence our habits, thinking, and attitudes. It is a proven principle for all aspects of life. We might even say it is how God knit us together as communal beings.

Now apply the principle to the Christian life. That is one of the reasons why Christian fellowship is indispensable in every culture. It's worth dying for.

A Word to the Church

For the church, fellowship happens around the word. The Bible is taught, and church life is impacted, even if ever so slightly, towards biblical fidelity in each gathering. It happens again and again, and Jesus's prayer, "Sanctify them by the truth, your word is truth" (John 17:17), is realized. Stop gathering and the process is interrupted.

Churching shapes us as people. When we listen to sermons together, we learn how to exegete the text, beeline to the gospel, and apply its precepts. When we pray together, we listen to how to articulate prayer. We sing together and experience others worshiping. In fellowship, one member shares his perspective of the text. Another gleans an insight she never saw before. We are shaping one another's lives. Newlyweds sit next to an older Christian couple married for seventy years (my church has one of these) and sees how they treat each other. Older members regain their sense of excitement and energy from watching a new believer devour the Scriptures. A struggling addict talks with a recovering addict about what got him through the hard days.

Church is the laboratory for biblical theology. It is the gospel's factory. Church is where we begin to apply what we read and hear. We hear the call to love one another, and we arrange a visit with a brother recovering from heart surgery or offer gas money to a sister who can barely afford the commute to work. We receive the word's exhortation to serve, and we find a ministry to help people out. Obedience to the Bible doesn't end with the church, but it often begins there.

Jacob asked me if he could serve the church by doing the jobs that nobody else wants to do. It wasn't long before he was cleaning the restrooms on Saturday mornings. He later roped his dad into helping him. Our church facility is in the downtown area of our city, next to city hall. At one point, we had a bit of an issue with the homeless sleeping on church property. That wasn't really a problem, except they had designated a particular spot on the property as their own public restroom. Jacob and his dad literally purchased a hazmat suit and cleaned it up for the church. They continue to do the jobs no one wants to do till this day, with a good attitude and a sense of humor. If I didn't fellowship with these two men, I would have never seen servant hearts quite like these. That has shaped me as a Christian.

I do not mean to make the process sound mundane. The Spirit of Jesus is at work in his church. The very presence of God manifests himself as Christians gather, worship, and fellowship (see John 17:23). The lengthy work of sanctification is done by the master craftsman himself, not just by mutual edification. Yet, the truth is he often uses tools to accomplish his work. We call them means of grace. The church is his chosen instrument towards the sanctification of his people.

This process is often slow and arduous. It isn't meant to be a sprint but a marathon. As we gather under the word, in fellowship with other Christians, slowly we experience transformation "from one degree of glory to another" (2 Cor 3:18).

Am I My Brother's Keeper?

We need accountability. The further we stray from gathering, the more we feel free to sin. Our hearts are prone to wander. We might wish we were more spiritually independent, but again, it is how God knit us together. Community brings about conformity, and some forms of conformity are good. Where sharing pornography, jokes about drunkenness, and mean-spirited snark are not accepted, people tend to fall in line. Rather than a curse, this corporate accountability is a godsend. It is the discipline we need to stay the course of faithfulness.

Conformity is in and of itself amoral. It is simply a reality of human experience. What we conform to is what makes it morally good or evil. This is not a magic bullet toward spiritual maturity. There are undoubtedly times when the church gets this wrong. Some congregations cause people to conform to norms that are neither biblical nor healthy. This conformity may be, for example, towards subtle forms of racism or ethnocentrism. It may be towards gossip and snobbery. Churches may fail to hold someone accountable due to either ignorance of a particular sin or apathy towards sin in general. There is the quip about a man who, when accused of ignorance and apathy, responded, "I don't know, and I don't care." Churches may feel the same.

In the net, fellowship shapes people towards Christian maturity more than any other factor, and by a long shot. As imperfect as the church is, it is the most effective means towards spiritual growth in the Christian life available to us. If a new Christian believer finds a church, her "chance" of enduring grows exponentially. If she does not, the likelihood of her faith faltering multiplies dangerously.

We will talk about the importance of cultural engagement and evangelism in a later chapter but suffice it to say now, when it comes to fellowship, the church community is your God-ordained context. No doubt, Jesus was "a friend of tax collectors and sinners" (Matt 11:19; Luke 7:34), but not in terms of Christian fellowship. His love for sinners was genuine, but so was his call for them to repent. How much time should we as Christians be spending with nonbelievers is a common pastoral question. The answer all depends on who is influencing whom. Spend as much time as you can, so long as you are the one drawing others to Christ and not the other way around. I have seen it more times than I care to admit that someone in the name of outreach falls back into "love with this present world" (2 Tim 4:10).

It's an old illustration, but I have yet to find a better one. When an ember falls from a campfire it slowly begins to burn out. In a brief time, it is cool enough to touch. Take it and throw it back into the blaze and it will reignite and produce flames with the rest. Spiritually, we are made for fellowship. We burn out without it. To answer Cain's humanity-old question, "Am I my brother's keeper?" (Gen 4:9), yes, and your brother or sister in Christ is yours.

The Discipline of the Church

There are times when a church needs to formally address sin. Just as people join the fellowship of the church, there is a time and place to disfellowship someone. The importance of this is such that some Reformers recognized church discipline as a third mark of a true church (behind teaching the word and the administration of the sacraments). A church needs to address sin through an often slow and always prayerful process (see Matt 18:15–20), and if necessary, to give someone the right *foot* of fellowship.

Excommunication has gotten a bad rap over the years, but it is the logical extension of accountability. What if a member is so recalcitrant in their sin that they cause disrepute and disorder in the whole church? Jesus's answer is to treat them as "a gentile or a tax collector" (Matt 18:17). As mentioned in the last chapter, this doesn't mean we hate them or even shun them. How did Jesus himself treat gentiles and tax collectors? He loved them but called them to repentance and faith. It is no surprise that the apostle recounting Jesus's teaching in this passage, Matthew, was himself a reformed tax collector.

How we treat the excommunicated has been a matter of some debate. Some have argued, like Menno Simons,[3] that those under church discipline are no longer welcomed to gathered worship. Others, like John Calvin, contended that for most church discipline the unrepentant should be allowed to gather, but it should be made clear they are not members in good standing of the church (e.g., they should be refused communion). How else will they be brought to conviction of their sin but by hearing the word preached? What is clear is the necessity of church discipline for the spiritual well-being of both the disciplined and the church. The intention behind this discipline is for everyone: for the sinner to find repentance and true faith; for the church, that sin might not spread throughout the fellowship; and for the witness of the gospel in the community.

While this all sounds harsh in principle, in practice few would want to do without it. Many of the shameful failures of the church in the last twenty-five years are due to a failure to discipline adequately. Should not the Catholic abusive priests have been outed and defrocked? Should not have those responsible for repeat financial indiscretions been exposed and prosecuted? Should not power-hungry pastors be addressed by courageous church board members, and if needed, be shown the door? A church without discipline is a frightening church to be part of given enough time (see 1 Cor 5:1–13). Wolves find their way into the flock, sure enough (Acts 20:29). There is a biblical way to unmask them.

---

3. Menno Simons (1496–1561) was an Anabaptist Reformer whose followers became known as the Mennonites.

Kissing the Wave

Charles Haddon Spurgeon is credited with saying, "I have learned to kiss the wave that throws me against the rock of ages."[4] Though the Spurgeon-esque quote is more likely a paraphrase of his rhetoric, it's a testimony heard over and again. Nothing is more powerful than suffering to force us to grow. Pain is God's megaphone, as C. S. Lewis argued in *The Problem of Pain*. "But pain insists upon being attended to. God whispers to us in our pleasures, speaks in our conscience, but shouts in our pain: it is His megaphone to rouse a deaf world."[5] The New Testament resonates with this theme throughout (see Rom 5:3–5; Jas 1:2–4). Even Jesus in his humanity, without sin "learned obedience through what he suffered" (Heb 5:8).

The church is filled with sinners, and sinners hurt one another. People inevitably say things that will hurt you, do things that cut you, and omit things (like "thank you" or "I'm sorry") that leave you feeling unappreciated. Most Christians have been hurt more by church members than by anyone outside the church. Talk to any group of longtime churchgoers and they will share stories of deep wounds inflicted upon them by the church. When considering proximity and time spent together, this is not surprising. Church families grow close, and it is those closest to us that can cause the most pain. The Psalms, the songs and prayers of the people of God, express the hearts of many church members:

> For it is not an enemy who taunts me—then I could bear it; it is not an adversary who deals insolently with me—then I could hide from him. But it is you, a man, my equal, my companion, my familiar friend. We used to take sweet counsel together; within God's house we walked in the throng. (Ps 55:12–14)

Was not Jesus himself hurt more by the betrayal and denial of his own disciples than the mocking of his enemies?

---

4. George, "Quotes Spurgeon Didn't Say," no. 5.
5. Lewis, *Complete C. S. Lewis*, 604.

Pastors are not immune to this pain. I've received anonymous emails filled with false accusations (I later noticed that much of the content of the emails was taken from the dialogue of a B-list movie). I have been told by leaving members that I am not a good pastor and by others that I am not a great preacher. One former member said I am a great preacher but not a good pastor. Another indicated that I am a good pastor, but he needs to leave to find better preaching! In my first few years, some members tried to organize a vote of no confidence. To be fair, I was making a lot of foolish mistakes back then. I still make them, just less often.

This may be hard to hear, but I think enduring this is part of God's purpose for the Christian life. It is easy to love the lovable; it is something special to love the unlovable (see Matt 5:46–47). Forgiveness is not possible where there is no sin, and grace has no meaning where there is no debt. This is no excuse for us to hurt one another, and anyone who sees it that way, shame on you. The day will come when we have fellowship without sin, but on this side of glory, even the pain that comes from fellow Christians has a purpose.

Floating down a river through the woods with nothing but your golden retriever and your L. L. Bean canoe is not so hard. There is no one to disagree with you, no one to challenge your opinions, and no one to talk over you when you are sharing something personal. Trust me, as an introvert, I can see the appeal! But a church of one is no church it all. Can you be faithful when surrounded by Christians starkly different than you and just as sinful as you are? Can you love them even when it is hard to do so? Can you stick it out together especially when you don't feel like it anymore?

I am not talking about abuse. There is a time to leave a church. More than that, there is a time to call the police and arrest a brother in Christ for his sin. When there is abuse of a child, you sin by not reporting to the governing authorities so they can lock up the perpetrator. Abuse comes in various forms, up to and including spiritual abuse, and simply enduring it is often the worst viable option, both for yourself and for the abuser. The abuser's path to repentance may be through the court room or a prison cell.

That said, there is no perfect church. It has been rightly said, if you have found a perfect church, leave immediately or you will ruin it with your own sin! Be sanctified by churching alongside these annoying, insensitive, careless spiritual siblings, even as they are sanctified by your peccadilloes and peculiarities. The church is a messy place. It won't be that way forever. For now, it is what it is meant to be. It is for your sanctification. Churching means committing to imperfect people who commit to an imperfect you.

Wise Counsel

Think about your own quirky personality traits that you hope others will overlook or even love you because of them. Think about your own sin that you hope others will forgive when you fail them or disappoint them. Then pray God gives you the strength to overlook, forgive, and love as you would have others do to you. Forgive as God has forgiven you. Start to fellowship with people different than you. Practice being the kind of Christian you want to be all the time while in the laboratory of the local church.

Discussion Questions

1. Why do you think Chinese Christians are willing to risk everything to fellowship with other Christians? Right now, would you risk your life just to be able to gather with fellow believers? Why or why not?

2. In what ways have you been shaped by your network of friends? Have you ever intentionally changed your network of friends in order to grow? How has spending time with other Christians changed you?

3. Have you ever witnessed church discipline? What was your reaction? Do you feel spiritually accountable to your church,

and is your church accountable to you? If so, how has this helped you in the Christian life?

4. How have you been hurt by your local church? Were you able to "kiss the wave," and eventually be thankful for the growth it brought about in you? How might you prepare a new church member for what to expect?

4

Authority Helps

THE NEED FOR SHEPHERDS

FOR THE FIRST TIME in our church's 260-year history (as far as I know), we offered a written ballot to straw poll whom the congregation would like to see as our newest elder. It was nonbinding, but we wanted to hear from the church body. To no one's surprise, the highest vote was for Ambrose. This was the man the current elders, including myself, saw as the most qualified candidate. Ambrose, a first-generation immigrant from Nigeria, had already gained a deep respect from the congregation, along with his lovely wife and his extraordinarily impressive family. He was also the first black elder in the church's extensive history, but that wasn't even part of the discussion.

The Baptist Church of Haverhill, Massachusetts, has an impressive history of Christian leadership. The church was founded by a New Light preacher named Hezekiah Smith, who served in the War of Independence as a chaplain under General George Washington.[1] He was an evangelist who planted churches all

---

1. Hezekiah Smith's biographer writes, "That Hezekiah Smith was acquainted with George Washington cannot be disputed. In an entry in his journal on August 2, 1778, Smith wrote, 'I preached a Sermon to our Brigade from Mal. 2:5. His Excellency Gen. Washington attended. I dined with him the same day.' Another dinner engagement with Washington occurred in late 1779." Broome, *Hezekiah Smith*, 137.

throughout New England. The second pastor, William Batchelder, led the church to support Adoniram Judson's mission to Burma after he became a Baptist on the sea voyage to Asia. Charlotte Atlee Rowe White came to faith under Batchelder's ministry and was baptized by him in our local river. Charlotte went on to be the first appointed female missionary from the United States or the United Kingdom.[2] Prolific hymn writer Stephen P. Hill pastored the church before going on to eventually become chaplain of the United States Senate. A hundred years after the church's founding, in 1865, during the dreadful Civil War, a youthful Augustus Strong took the pastorate. A. H. Strong went on to become president of Rochester Theological Seminary in New York and to write his widely used, three-volume *Systematic Theology*.[3] The church stood firmly on the side of abolitionism. Less than sixty years later, we were happy to add an elder like Ambrose to the spiritual leadership pedigree of the church.

The Lord added Ambrose. Ambrose was a shepherd before he was appointed an elder. People in the congregation witnessed his character, listened to his teaching, and looked to his leadership before they recognized him as an elder. The church didn't make him a leader; they ordained a man the Lord had already appointed as one.

Celebrities and Pastors

We are skeptical of authority, more so than any previous generation. It's in our DNA as Americans. We are after all born of a revolution from the tyrant King George III. In the last 250 years, our antiauthoritarian sentiments have only grown stronger. Reinforcing it, we have seen political figures get suspiciously wealthy, the "me too" movement expose business leaders and movie moguls, and social media billionaires playing god behind the curtain. But is this defiant attitude healthy?

---

2. Trulson, *Charlotte Atlee White Rowe*.
3. Strong, *Systematic Theology*.

Authority Helps

The church has sadly been no exception to this abuse of power. One church leader after another has fallen from grace. I am hesitant to mention any names lest this paragraph be outdated before it is even published. Celebrity pastors have lived up to their oxymoronic title (for isn't a pastor one who leads people to *celebrate* the Lord?) and have left a bad taste in everybody's mouth. The respect given to clergy across the board has declined steeply. They are sometimes categorized alongside shady used car salesmen and disreputable attorneys.

This is stark in New England, where the Roman Catholic child abuse scandal still looms ominously over churches. While the diocese was not alone in their diabolical scheming, they are the spotlight example of the depths of hell unleashed by corrupt authority. Our inclination is to throw out the baby with the bathwater and be done with church authority entirely. While I can understand the sentiment, anarchy is the worst of all options. Lord of the Flies is no improvement over Big Brother. The Bible describes this spirit of anarchy: "In those days there was no king in Israel. Everyone did what was right in his own eyes" (Judg 17:6; 21:25).

Legit to Submit

In the Bible, it is fundamental that God holds authority over all things. What is more, he sets up lesser authorities over various spheres of life. The role of the state is to bear the sword (e.g., Rom 13:1–7); the place of a parent is to discipline without exasperating (e.g., Eph 6:1–4); and the church is to be led by mature elders (e.g., Acts 14:23). To spurn these authorities is to do yourself harm.

There are limits to earthly authority. No earthly rule is absolute. God gives temporary and limited authority under heaven, and we are responsible to submit only as far as that authority is granted and so long as that authority is acting morally.[4] Civil dis-

---

4. "Churches should not wield the sword. Governments should not decide who gets baptized. Politicians generally should not tell pastors which doctrines to hold. Parents generally should not forbid children from seeking morally legitimate and necessary medical treatment. And schools generally should not

obedience is not only allowed but at times demanded. When lesser authorities defy the authority of God himself, we defy them. There is a time to remind them of the words of Peter and John, "Whether it is right in the sight of God to listen to you rather than to God, you must judge" (Acts 4:19).

While in Eisenach, Germany, I had the opportunity to visit Wartburg Castle. The castle has its own rich history, but it is most known for the eleven-month residency of the Reformer Martin Luther. After Luther's bold defiance against the corrupt medieval Catholic Church at the Diet of Worms, and his ever-resonating words, "Here I stand, I cannot do otherwise,"[5] it was assumed he would be arrested and put to death. Instead, he was kidnapped and whisked off into hiding by his own German elector, Frederick III, in defiance of the Holy Roman Emperor, Charles V. There in hiding, and going by the pseudonym Knight George, Luther translated the New Testament from Greek into German. Both Luther and Frederick rebelled against their authorities by submitting to a higher authority—namely, the word of God.

Character First

Scripturally speaking, a pastor (Gr. *poime*) is an overseer (Gr. *episkopos*) is an elder (Gr. *presbyteros*). The titles are almost interchangeable. We may parse out the differences today with various ecclesiastical roles like minister, bishop, or lay elder, but we can jettison that parsing when we come to the New Testament. Essentially what these people do is lead a church.

We are given the qualifications for such church leaders in two primary passages: 1 Tim 3:1–7 and Titus 1:5–9. The lists are extraordinary for their ordinariness. They are composed almost entirely of basic Christian morality: good family men, not drunks or violent, kind, and hospitable.[6] They list what we should expect

---

undermine a parents' authority concerning what to teach their children." Leeman, *Authority*, 77.

5. Bainton, *Here I Stand*, 144.

6. The one notable exception to the list of character qualification is the

from any Christian person. What is called for is character above all else. If you aren't a model of Christian character, then your talents are irrelevant to the office of pastor. I love that.

To be in authority is a call to serve those we oversee. There is a reason we call political leaders *ministers*—that is, servants. Their authority is such that it is meant to serve those submitting to them. Jesus modeled leadership as a powerful form of servanthood. "The Son of Man came not to be served but to serve, and to give his life as a ransom for many" (Matt 20:28).

It is better to have no one in leadership of a church than a person without the necessary character qualifications to be in that office. I will go a step further; it is better for a church to close its doors than to compromise on this principle and put an immoral person in place. They will do more damage to the kingdom by compromising on this in order to keep the doors open than could ever be lost by closing them. As a pastor, this is a mistake I have made all too often: rushing someone into leadership whom I do not know well enough, or trying to force fit someone into a position who does not have the temperament or integrity. While there is a learning curve to spiritual leadership, for sure (the only way you get wise old pastors is by allowing them to be foolish young pastors for a few years!), this is entirely different than ignoring the character qualifications. Even with this learning curve, we should be careful: "He must not be a recent convert, or he may become puffed up with conceit and fall into the condemnation of the devil" (1 Tim 3:6).

Shepherded

The Bible gives us shepherds for our own good. They equip the saints (Eph 4:11–16). Here is one more reason why churching matters in the Christian life. Gathering with a bunch of buddies around a campfire to talk Bible, however rewarding and uplifting,

---

ability to teach, which is a gifting or competency qualification. Understandably, while an ability to teach is not expected of every mature Christian, it is expected of those who are responsible to shepherd and care for the church.

leaves no room for the role of spiritual authority. A campus minister might prove a good evangelist, but does he provide a shepherd for your soul? A stand-alone small group might be led by a phenomenal teacher, but does she have the authority to use the rod and staff? If there are no functioning overseers in the group, there is no church.

Being under authority teaches us humility. John Calvin believed that the fifth commandment, honor your parents, was a way of addressing all submission to authority. Learning to submit to parents is good prep for submitting to God and the authorities appointed by him. Even Jesus submits to a higher authority functionally within the Triune God: "The head of every man is Christ, the head of a wife is her husband, and the head of Christ is God" (1 Cor 11:3). Submission may be a dirty curse word in our culture, but in the Bible, it is a gracious blessing towards spiritual maturity.

To submit to those called to serve you spiritually is not only appropriate (e.g., Gal 6:6; 1 Tim 5:17, Heb 13:7), it is also to your own benefit: "Let them do this with joy and not with groaning, for that would be of no advantage to you" (Heb 13:17). Spiritual leaders keep watch over your soul and will give an accounting for you in the end. Let them help you make it across the finish line.

Submission is part of churching. To be humble enough to see the need for spiritual authority over your life is to swim upstream. If you want to be truly radical, join a church and submit to leadership. People will think you went crazy! Submitting to good authorities may be the most countercultural thing a Christian can do in this generation. It is also a crucial means of grace. The unyielding, rebellious, and obstinate heart will hit a spiritual ceiling; the humble, teachable, and corrigible will soar past it.

Members and Membership

None of this is to say that clergy are what is most important for the church, or even more important. The picture in the New Testament is of a church with diverse gifting: "We, though many, are one body in Christ, and individually members one of another" (Rom 12:5).

AUTHORITY HELPS

The church body is as diverse as the human body, and its members all essential for the body to function correctly (see 1 Cor 12). It is only to say that part of that body is church leadership, and that some are called to be "the shepherds and teachers, to equip the saints for the work of ministry, for building up the body of Christ" (Eph 4:11–12). To neglect them is like trying to function without a tailbone or a voice box. It can be done but not without problems.

Those with spiritual *gifts* of leadership fill *offices* of leadership in the church. This was a way of ensuring that the local church would be well cared for in the long run. That is why the early missionaries were eager to get these folks into office: "And when they had appointed elders for them in every church, with prayer and fasting they committed them to the Lord in whom they had believed" (Acts 14:23). This is why Paul told Titus to stay put until this job was done: "This is why I left you in Crete, so that you might put what remained into order, and appoint elders in every town as I directed you" (Tit 1:5).

This is also the spirit behind church membership. Like that of a human body, each Christian is to play her role in the service of the church according to her particular gifting. The recognition of such commitment and service is what it means to become a "member." Some churches opt to not use the word member, as it has come to carry unhelpful baggage (country clubs and bulk grocers co-opted it!), but to discard the concept of membership is to blur lines I don't think we want to blur. If you are a church that enjoys visitors of different beliefs and faiths on a regular basis, like most churches I would hope, how do you distinguish who is the church and who is not? We should welcome the evangelistic opportunity when "an unbeliever or an outsider enters" (1 Cor 14:24), but for there to be an outsider, there needs to be some sense of what the inside is. Surely not anyone who shows up on a given Sunday is the church. How does a church remove someone if there is no recognized body from which to remove him? Written rolls or not, the early church had members.

Consumer Christianity

The church has depended far too much on a consumer culture to attract attenders. Instead of calling people to costly discipleship, which includes submission ultimately to God and his word but by extension to a local church, the church has depended on worldly marketing techniques. It has sought to make the gospel more appealing to felt needs and the Christian faith more attractive to the flesh. Just show up at one of the many service times the church offers every weekend and let us entertain you with SNL-like skits, TED Talk-like messages, all while in a concert-like atmosphere. None of these are necessarily wrong, but what is the motive behind this approach to corporate worship? With this approach, the church has unwittingly (or maybe in some cases wittingly) created consumers instead of disciples.

One of the Bible's most common designations for Christians is servants or, more starkly translated, slaves (Gr. *doulos*) of Jesus Christ. Christian leaders in particular opted for this designation. It was not only the apostle Paul's favorite self-identification (e.g., Rom 1:1), even Jesus's own brothers opted to use it (Jas 1:1; Jude 1). If nothing else, a slave is one who submits. Even megachurches are starting to see the danger of where this consumerism has led us. "Contrast the image of consumer with a much different biblical image that Scripture uses to describe followers," writes Kyle Idleman. "The Bible would describe a follower as a 'slave.' That is the exact opposite of a consumer."[7] *Fans* of Jesus pick and choose what they want to cheer on. *Followers* seek to live in obedience to his calling.

If we spurn all forms of submission to authority, in time we will find ourselves in a place far from Christianity, deep in the recesses of anarchy and individualism.

---

7. Idleman, *Not a Fan*, 149.

Wise Counsel

Seek out a wise pastor or elder at your church that you've grown to respect. Ask to meet with him. Don't come looking to place any demands or requirements on him, but just let him know you are happy to have him as a shepherd. You want to learn from him, and you are open to any advice or wise counsel he might be able to offer you. As you get his advice, feel free to disagree with his counsel but do so only after carefully considering why he would want to guide you in that direction. Pray for him to shepherd you and others in the church well.

Discussion Questions

1. What is your view of authority? How have you experienced bad authorities in your own life? Have you experienced bad authority in the church particularly? Does this make you skeptical to ever want to submit to authority again?

2. How is God the authority over all? What makes him worthy of being such an authority? What lesser authorities has he set up for human beings for our good? When, do you think, is it right for us to oppose them?

3. Why do you think Christian character is the most important quality for church leadership in the New Testament? What "celebrity pastor" failure has shocked you the most? How did his or her failure affect you personally?

4. What steps can you take to begin to submit to church authority in your life? What would change in your life if you did? How do you think this will affect your spiritual growth as a Christian? How do you feel about membership?

5

Ordinary Ministry

A CASE FOR SACRAMENTS

I WAS TRAVELING AROUND Israel in July of 2023, a few months before the vicious attacks of October 7th. I had the opportunity to stay in a kibbutz, or at least the hotel portion of the property. This was my second trip to the Holy Land, so rather than go see the traditional sites again, I went to lesser visited spots like the caves of Beit Guvron and the Crusader Chapel in Abu Ghosh. We also stopped for hummus and falafel at an Arab restaurant, which was out of this world.

    I did make one return visit to the Church of the Holy Sepulcher. This is the traditional site of Jesus's death, burial, and resurrection. My first visit here was underwhelming as large crowds and a sizable tour group made it almost impossible to take time to reflect. This time I snuck away by myself to the lowest accessible level of the church building. It was below ground, with rock walls protected by plexiglass. It was eerily quiet. For a few moments, I could feel something sacred about the place. Whether or not this is the actual place of Jesus's burial, we may never know for sure.[1] Even if it is, he was only buried here for three days! However, deep in the depths of that old church building built in AD 335, the echo

---

1. There is a rival site for the resurrection, the Garden Tomb, which is also well worth the visit.

of the ages resonated through the stones. Generation after generation of Christian pilgrims journeyed here to contemplate and worship the risen King.

I think I understood more clearly what it means to experience the sacred. The sacred is not mere superstition; it is the ordinary saturated with symbolism. Symbols matter. This is why burning a flag stirs emotions high. It is not about the value of dyed cloth. I would never spit on a cross—not because of love for bronze but because the symbolism would be deeply offensive. We define ourselves by our symbols. To see through them and define reality as merely the physical or natural is to be spiritually blind. "If you see through everything, then everything is transparent," Lewis wrote in *The Abolition of Man*. "But a wholly transparent world is an invisible world. To 'see through' all things is the same as not to see."[2]

Ordinary Worship

The word ordinance comes from the Latin *ordinantia* from which we also get the word ordinary or orderly. The idea behind it is that which is ordained (ordered) by Jesus Christ. High church liturgies prefer the term sacrament, from *sacramentum* meaning sign of the sacred. While at first these two designations seem almost contradictory, in practice they are not. In the ordinances, the ordinary becomes the sacred as the sacrament is infused with meaning and symbolism. Whether or not there is more going on in these ordinances than merely the symbolic I will leave to your own study and reflection, but there is certainly not less. Because Jesus has ordered us to practice them, they are now sacred for us. In baptism, water is not just water but a symbol of the cleansing of sin. In the Lord's Table, the bread and wine are not miniscule morsels of food, they are fused with the symbol of Jesus's own body and blood. The ordinary becomes sacred in the corporate worship of the church.

When Christians gather, they engage not just in fellowship but in worship. The expression of that worship often includes

---

2. Lewis, *Complete C. S. Lewis*, 730. These are the final lines of the book.

prayers, songs, and the ministry of the word. In addition, the ordinary worship of the Christian church should include baptism and the Lord's Table. The Reformers defined a true church as a gathering that both rightly teaches the word of God and rightly administers the ordinances. One of the key elements of churching that is being lost in the dechurching of the West is the importance and spiritual value of this administration.

I grew up Roman Catholic. That is pretty much true of everyone from New England.[3] After leaving the Church of Rome, I went through an anti-tradition phase, as many do. The more casual the better. The smells and bells were distractions from worship in spirit and truth, so I figured. I hope I have matured a bit from that dismissive attitude. Just as tradition can be a stumbling block to genuine worship, so an obsession with organic worship can become an idol in its own way. Styles of worship tend to reveal more about personal preferences than theological convictions. Sure, high church liturgies might bring out a certain reverence for God, but are we not also called to address the sovereign Lord as *Abba*? Yes, low church worship shows the intimacy we have with our dear brother Jesus, but is he not also the Son of Man who sits beside the Ancient of Days?

The real question is whether we are worshiping in the way the Bible prescribes. Nothing is said about clerical robes and special collars, nor about jeans and T-shirts, but the ordinances are set out as nonnegotiables for Christians, and the primary context for their practice is the local church.

Baptism

The instruction to baptize and celebrate the Lord's Table both come directly from Jesus. They are not the product of centuries of church history. No doubt, the details of how they are practiced has morphed and evolved from culture to culture through the ages (shall we use chalices or tiny clear plastic cups?), but the essence

---

3. Jackson, *New England*, 29.

and symbolism of them has remained a constant. Jesus's final command in the Gospel according to Matthew, often called the Great Commission, was to make disciples. One of the means to accomplish this was "baptizing them in the name of the Father, the Son and the Holy Spirit" (Matt 28:19). As seen in the book of Acts, the disciples did just that, baptizing individuals (e.g., Acts 8:38) and households (e.g., Acts 16:33) as they came to faith.

The mode and recipient of baptism have long been debated. Some churches sprinkle water from a baptismal font; others immerse down by the river. Some churches baptize the infants of Christian believers, while credobaptists require a profession of faith, necessitating a coming of age. Regardless, in each case the symbol of baptism includes cleansing from sin and reception into the covenant community. To be baptized is to publicly confess for yourself (or in some traditions for your child) a death to an old self and a resurrection to a new life united to Jesus Christ (see Rom 6:1–4). It is an initiation into the faith.

Some might argue that we do not need the church to do that. All you need is two individuals. One Christian can baptize another sure enough. I do wonder how often this ordinance is employed in this way in a dechurched setting, but even if so, it still misses the mark. Baptism is a public profession to the body of Christ and, ideally, to a watching world. No one baptizes herself for a reason. Like the apostle Paul's call to find Ananias in Damascus before being baptized (see Acts 9:10–19), so no Christian goes it alone. It is only when a new believer is connected to other Christians that he is to be baptized.

It is no wonder that, right or wrong, the early church insisted upon a lengthy period (up to two years) before baptism for catechumens or new converts. The church was to protect against false conversions and ensure a true profession. Even Jesus's brief instructions on baptism include "in the name of the Father and of the Son and of the Holy Spirit" (Matt 28:19). The Trinitarian formula is telling. It is not the *names* (plural) that one is baptized into, as in polytheism. It is in the one Name, representing a single Being. Yet neither is it only in one person of the Trinity, say the Son, dispelling for example modalism, a belief that God simply appears in the various modes of Father, Son, or Spirit. In his command to baptize, Jesus establishes the essential definition of the Trinity: one being with three persons. The church acts as a necessary safeguard for sound doctrine even in the act of baptism.

In Jesus's commission, baptism precedes the *ongoing* didactic ministry of the church, "teaching them to obey all that I have commanded them" (Matt 28:20). It is an initiation. If baptism is a symbol (again, at minimum), and that symbol is initiation into the Christian community and the process of discipleship, what use is the symbol without the Christian community into which one is initiated? If there is no church that someone is becoming part of, there is no need for an initiation symbol.

Admittedly, baptism seems freer than Communion when it comes to when and where we practice it. The Ethiopian eunuch was baptized by Philip with no church in sight (Acts 8:36–40). Similarly, Paul baptized the Philippian jailer and his household without waiting for the church in Philippi to be fully formed (Acts 16:25–34). Missionaries sometimes find themselves in similar situations. I have talked to some who have baptized a new Christian believer and didn't have any native church to direct him to after doing so. It would seem intuitive, however, that if a viable church community existed, it would witness the new believer's public profession of faith. This is undoubtedly the way the generation of Christians immediately after the book of Acts applied the practice.[4] With the Lord's Table, on the other hand, it is the New Testament itself that requires the local church's involvement, as we will see.

As a Baptist pastor, I love baptisms. They are my favorite ceremonies to officiate—more so than weddings or funerals. We often have a group baptized on Easter Sunday each year, a practice common through much of church history. I remember one particular year when it struck me: This Irish-Korean pastor was baptizing a Puerto Rican *hermana* and a Latvian *masa* with the symbol of

---

4. Take, for example, the instructions of the Didache later in the first century on how the church is to officiate baptisms for new converts.

cleansing from sin and union with the resurrected Jesus Christ. Disciples were being made of all nations, and our local church got to witness it. The Great Commission was clearly at work two millennia after Jesus gave the command!

The Lord's Table

The Last Supper. Holy Communion. Eucharist. There are lots of names for this ordinance, but all represent the same sacrament. With the symbol of broken bread and poured out wine, we "proclaim the Lord's death until he comes" (1 Cor 11:26).

We again find ourselves in the arena of controversy over an ordinance. What is the exact nature of what is happening when we partake of the Lord's Table? Answers range from transubstantiation (the bread and wine becoming the physical body and blood of Jesus), to the so-called memorial view, to a couple of views in-between. What can be agreed upon is celebrating the Lord's Table is no *less* than a symbol of Jesus's death for our sins, done "in remembrance" of him. When Christians gather to receive Communion, they are commemorating the sacrifice of Jesus crucified for us.

During the Passover, the Jewish people remembered with vivid symbols their exodus from Egypt and salvation from the angel of death. Jesus takes this very same ceremony and two of its elements and infuses them with new symbolic meaning. As a new covenant in his blood, it now points to our rescue from the slavery of sin and salvation from the impending judgment of God. In Passover, the table set for the Israelites invited extended family to enjoy the sacramental meal together as a remembrance. For Jesus, it was his "earnest desire" (Luke 22:15) to celebrate it with his new spiritual family. To be welcome at the Table of Jesus is not only to be in fellowship with him but with your brothers and sisters. It is Communion as well as Eucharist (i.e., thanksgiving). We are to come to the Table "discerning the body" (1 Cor 11:29).

The church in Corinth was a test case in how to mess up Communion! We learn more about early eucharistic practices from their debacle than anywhere else in the Bible except the Last

Supper itself. Some Corinthians would eat without waiting for the rest of the assembly. Others would go hungry, not able to afford the food. Some would even drink so much wine they would get drunk from it! Their lack of recognition of the unity of the church body led to many becoming "weak or ill," and even some dying. To take communion without a recognition of the church body was to eat and drink judgment on oneself (see 1 Cor 11:27–34). To approach the Lord's Table with no love for the body of Christ is emblematic of our view of Jesus himself.

Where has dechurching left us when it comes to the Lord's Table? Many dechurched Christians simply discard the symbol as unnecessary for the genuine Christian life. Others may choose to celebrate it in the context of a gathering of friends. While this might maintain the symbolism of remembrance of Jesus's death, it is woefully lacking when it comes to discerning the body of Christ, a synonym for the church.

Ceremonial, Not Ceremonialism

It is often thought that Jesus taught an anti-ceremonial approach to worship. He condemned the ceremonies of the Pharisees: ritualistic washings, extensive Sabbath regulations, and rabbinic traditions surrounding divorce. He envisioned an approach to God that was more intimate, casual, and unassuming.

While it is true that Jesus condemned the ceremonialism of the religious leaders of his day, he did not spurn the legitimate ceremonies of the Torah. He was circumcised and went to the temple for worship. He celebrated Passover, Yom Kippur, and the Festival of Booths. More than that, he is the one who calls us to the ceremonies of baptism and the Lord's Table. The difference is these ceremonies all point *back* to him. Those that came before work as shadows whose substance is found in Christ (see Col 2:16–17), and those we now practice call our hearts and minds to recall the gospel repeatedly.

Think of the narrative of Scripture. We have two options; one does justice to the story of the Bible while the other distorts it. In the anti-ceremonial view, God gives his people the Torah outlining numerous ceremonies that assist in the worship of the Lord, then Jesus comes along and tells them these are all useless and unhelpful and calls them to casual worship. In option two, God gives us the Torah, and Jesus defines all these ceremonies as consummated in his life, death, and resurrection, condemning those that are man made and any idolatry of ceremonialism (see Matt 15:1–9). He then calls us to new ceremonies that more clearly point us to himself. The first wrecks the narrative of Scripture in favor of a modern approach to worship. The other convicts us to see our failure to take seriously the ceremonies Jesus designated and Christians have embraced through the centuries. Whether the ceremony takes place in a cathedral or a house church, it should be part of the ordinary worship of the church.

Weddings and Funerals

While weddings and funerals appear in Scripture (see for example the wedding at Cana in John 2), there is no clear command to practice them in a certain way. Marriage is good, and death is the great transition for Christians, but as to how we should commemorate these key events, there is a great deal of freedom. I've officiated weddings with a dozen people in a backyard, and I've officiated weddings where wedding planners were planning out the ceremony to the minute, literally. There is no prescribed way to do a wedding or a funeral.

We should be grateful for this freedom! When I officiate a wedding, I always let the couple know that something is likely to go wrong. Just accept that from the outset. It happens at pretty much every wedding. It may be something small, like getting the giggles during the wedding vows, or maybe a little more serious, like a bridesmaid fainting (note, the wedding party stays put, and a designated nurse checks her out), but it is going to happen. Sometimes I am the source of the problem, forgetting to tell people to sit when they are supposed to or messing up my part of the marriage certificate twice in a row . . . oops. It's okay. That is part of what will make your wedding unique. The important thing is doing the actual vows. In the immortal words of *The Princess Bride*, if you didn't say "I do," than you didn't do it. The rest is just tradition.

A good rule of thumb is to allow all our religious ceremonies to point us to Jesus. A Christian wedding celebrates the symbol, with groom and bride, of the union of Jesus and his church (e.g., Eph 5:22–33). The wedding is a living parable. Every wedding should make us yearn for the "marriage supper of the lamb" (Rev 19:9). What better way to add kingdom value than to surround yourselves with your church community.

A Christian funeral reminds people of our eternal life in union with Jesus Christ (e.g., 2 Cor 5:1–10). As a pastor, I have officiated an inordinate number of funerals due to some unique circumstances (e.g., having a funeral director as a church member). Last I checked my records, it was well over a hundred. My goal for these services is to foster "a peace of God, that surpasses all understanding" (Phil 4:7). It is a call towards the hope of heaven to the bereaved. We say goodbye with tears in our eyes and are given one more glimpse of what is to come for all of us. It also calls our attention forward to the return of Jesus. Here is the point: let your final act of churching be to give your spiritual family a reminder of the blessed hope. Let it bring their hearts to say, one more time, "Come, Lord Jesus" (Rev 22:20). Weddings and funerals are not ordinances per se, but they are opportunities for kingdom advancement.

The Music of the Church

For the church, the connection between music and worship is so strong the two are often used indistinguishably, as in the words "Let's turn our hearts now to worship," as the choir or worship team takes the stage. The rich history of Christian hymnody is beautiful. Even our culture cannot help but sing them around Christmas time! Secular movies might have "Joy to the World" or "Silent Night" as part of their score or even include the vocals. Beyond Christmas, the lyrics and tune of "Amazing Grace" and

"Joyful, Joyful We Adore Thee" ("Ode to Joy") are so familiar you would be hard-pressed to find someone not familiar with them.

Modern praise music has also become exceptionally good. I am not one to diminish one for the other. At one point, every classic hymn was a modern song. It may be hard to think of Isaac Watts as innovative and controversial to be sung in churches, but his music was when it first came into usage. As far as content goes, I would put the lyrics of, say, "In Christ Alone" by the Gettys or "Yet Not I, but Through Christ in Me" by CityAlight on par with any classic hymn theologically. I realize, even by mentioning these songs, I am dating myself. We should hope that fresh and diverse gospel-centered music will continue to be produced till Christ returns.

There is however one attribute that sets apart genuinely great Christian worship music: congregational singing. What has made the music of Christianity so meaningful is that it was designed as the music of the church. It was meant to be sung together. Whether it is singing a Civil War era classic about how firm our foundation is or a worship number about the beautiful name of Jesus, it reaches a new level when sung together by a Christian community. It is not that you cannot sing and worship on your own; I hope you do, often and loudly! But that is something entirely different than singing with the saints.[5]

Christian worship has included "psalms and hymns and spiritual songs" (Eph 5:19; Col 3:16) for as long as churches have worshiped. It would be hard to imagine a church service with no music and no singing—around the world or throughout the ages. Martin Luther famously said, "Next after theology I give to music the highest place and the greatest honor."[6] Worship by music has a way of almost bypassing the head and affecting the heart. Luther

---

5. If I could put out a challenge to Christian songwriters, it would be to write more lyrics with "we" and "our" rather than "I" and "my." This critique is true of hymns, as much as praise songs, which for whatever reasons were also often written from the first-person singular perspective (e.g., John Newton's "saved a wretch like me," in "Amazing Grace" or Robert Robinson's "tune my heart to sing thy grace" in "Come, Thou Fount of Every Blessing").

6. Luther, quoted in Bainton, *Here I Stand*, 267.

also writes, "Music is to be praised as second only to the word of God because by her are all the emotions swayed."[7]

I think if I stopped gathering with the church and just sat home by myself on Sundays, I would miss the congregational singing most immediately (as an introvert, missing the fellowship would come a little later). It is not that I sing well; I don't. It is not that my church sings so well; they do all right. It is that when we sing together, we worship in a way I cannot replicate on my own. To worship this way, we need the church.

The Extraordinary Ordinary

To be considered ordinary today is almost an insult. We don't want to be ordinary people with ordinary experiences. We want to live our best life now, with extraordinary worship and spiritual high followed by spiritual high. The truth is most of our lives are lived in the ordinary. We get up in the morning, go through our routines to get ready, go to class or work, and come home. Then we might watch some TV, eat some dinner with family, or go out with friends. Punctuating our ordinary days are vacations or birthdays that break up the norm. They are often fun and exciting, but they are short-lived. Then we return to our ordinary.

Spiritual growth comes mostly during the ordinary, not the extraordinary. If you want to get in shape, one long day at the gym will do little more than make you sore. Structure a workout into your schedule three times a week, and you will see results. Make it part of the ordinary. I have been a gym goer since I was fifteen—so for over thirty years. My kids call me an "old head." One of the patterns I see at my gym is how busy it gets in January, and how quickly it dwindles down again shortly after New Year's resolutions wear off. It spikes again around April or May, as the summer approaches and people want a beach body. And again, it dies down shortly after. For the middle-aged guys like me, the only way we are going to get and stay in shape is to make workouts a weekly discipline.

---

7. Luther, quoted in Bainton, *Here I Stand*, 268.

Ordinary Ministry

This goes for nearly all areas of growth. If you want to learn a musical instrument, or master a new subject like WWII history, or take up a new hobby like restoring cars, one extraordinary event will not usually make a difference. Daily piano lessons, reading a chapter a night in a history book, or tinkering in the garage after work will change your lifestyle. It may take a year or two before you really see the difference, but you will. Ironically, if you want to break out of the ordinary, the answer is not the extraordinary but to begin to alter your ordinary day!

The Christian life is no different. If you want to *mature* in the faith, it is not a single retreat or a three-day conference that will make the bulk of difference. They have their place, and I have personally benefited from conferences and retreats, but they can never replace the ongoing ordinary worship of the church. When these temporary events act as surrogates for the church, they can become a cancer to spiritual growth. "Nothing is easier than to stimulate the glow of fellowship in a few days of life together," writes Dietrich Bonhoeffer. "But nothing is more fatal to the sound, sober, brotherly fellowship of everyday life."[8]

It will be the regular, consistent, ordinary ministry of your local church that will do the trick. It takes time and commitment— "over years of everyday exposure to and participation in the communion of Christ with his people," Michael Horton writes. "It's precisely the ordinary ministry, week-in and week-out, that provides sustained growth and encourages the roots to grow deep."[9] Go be with your church on Sundays; listen to the word preached, get baptized and witness baptisms, take communion, and sing together in worship. In time, the ordinary saturated with the sacred will transform you.

Churching creates a rhythm of the Christian life that strengthens faith perpetually, consistently, regularly, like a muscle at the gym.

---

8. Bonhoeffer, *Life Together*, 39.
9. Horton, *Ordinary*, 23.

CHURCHING

Wise Counsel

Make plans to get baptized if you haven't yet. Don't rush it. Speak with the pastor or a church leader and ask what the process is. Take communion seriously. There was a time in my own life that I was feeling spiritually dry. I wasn't getting much out of the sermons. The Lord's Table was like water to my thirsty soul. It consistently preached the gospel to me, even if I felt like the sermon failed to do so. Do not underestimate the spiritual importance of engaging in the symbol of the Lord's Table with your church family, even when—especially when—you don't feel like it. Sing with the church.

Discussion Questions

1. How would you define the sacred? Have you ever had an experience where you sensed you were experiencing something sacred? How did you react? How has that experience affected your faith?

2. If you have been baptized, describe your experience. If you were an infant at the time, do you now attribute value and meaning to that event in your life? If you haven't been baptized, what are your reservations about it?

3. Do you regularly take the Lord's Table with your church family? Why or why not? How can we make sure it does not become mere ceremonialism? What role has it played in your faith over your life?

4. If you are not married and are hoping to be so, are you planning to celebrate your wedding with your church? Why or why not? Would you want your funeral to be commemorated with your church? What value might it have for your church?

6

Join the Party

DISTINCT FOR THE WORLD

I AM SURROUNDED BY Brazilians. That is not a complaint; it's a privilege! One of my best friends is a Brazilian pastor, Lierte Soares. My church shares our space with a large Brazilian congregation—and not the one he pastors. I serve as provost of an organization called the Multiplication Center that hosts a group of Brazilians for an immersive week of ministry training in New England. I've been invited to speak for one of the most influential pastors in Brazil, as his friend. I speak only a handful of Portuguese words and have no ethnic background south of the equator, but I love Brazilians! By some accounts, Brazil is the most religious country in the world. No less than 87 percent consider themselves Christians.[1] Churches are full and active throughout the Land of the Holy Cross.

Cross over the Atlantic to Sweden. Whereas Brazil is the most religious nation, Sweden is recognized as the least religious country in the world. While there are some evangelical churches in Sweden, many have a predominantly immigrant membership.[2]

---

1. "According to the 2010 census, the most recently available data from official sources, 65 percent of the population is Catholic, 22 percent Protestant, 8 percent irreligious (including atheists, agnostics, and deists), and 2 percent Spiritists." US Department of State, "2022 Report," sec. 1.

2. I was looking to connect with missionaries in Sweden and was informed that currently the International Mission Board (IMB) of the Southern Baptist

Christianity dates to the days of the Vikings in Sweden, with the conversion of King Olaf in the eleventh century. Indeed, historically, "the end of Viking raiding followed on from conversion to Christianity."[3] Today, the land of the Swedish Baptists has become predominately irreligious. I was interviewed by two Swedish high schoolers doing a report on politics in the United States. We had an enjoyable conversation, but I could tell that much of what I shared about the Christian faith sounded foreign to them. I was like a tropical bird in the Amazon.

While fewer of them, and smaller in size, faithful churches in Sweden are just as characterized by warm fellowship and active worship as the churches in Brazil. The surrounding culture may be radically different in each country, which may affect the types of ministries they engage in and the way they approach missions and evangelism, but the church is the church is the church.

The Parish Model

For much of church history, Christians have employed the parish model of ministry. A parish is a geographical district in which a local church is responsible to minister. With the explosion of free churches, the parish model has been nearly phased out. While there were certainly problems with it, there is something to be said of this approach. For one, it put the onus of responsibility on a local congregation to do its part in serving its greater community. Where your church is located (the people, not the building), you are called to reach and minister.

Since a church is composed of a group of people who meet in a particular locale, that locale depends on them to act as witnesses in their community. We are to love our neighbors in our own neighborhood. While our neighbors are not limited to those within geographical reach, especially in this modern globalized world, there is a certain priority to a person in need standing right

---

Convention does not currently have a single missionary affiliation in Sweden. I am hopeful for this to change soon.

3. Whittock, *Vikings*, 131.

in front of us. The people we work with, shop with at the grocery store, and whose kids sit next to ours in the classroom surely have a priority in our Christian witness and our church's ministry.

We are called to engage with Christian love. Did not the apostles feel the need to reach out to Jerusalem before heading to Spain? Before we conquer the world for Christ, we should consider how we are doing with downtown. If each church took seriously its call to care for its greater community, the rest of the Great Commission would be a breeze. Besides, the world has come to us. It is not unusual for a neighborhood to be composed of immigrants from around the world, with family connections in nations globally.

Especially in urban settings, even if only from people visiting on a given Sunday, a church might have an influence across the globe. As I write this, last Sunday we had an Anglican priest visiting us from the village of Umuofor in the state of Okija Anambra, Nigeria, and a Brazilian pastor visiting us from São Paulo, Brazil. The love and welcome the church showed them I hope gives them some encouragement as they return home, even as we were blessed to have them with us.

The problem with the parish model is sometimes the next-door neighbors take precedence over the church family. Pastors become primarily civil servants rather than shepherds of the flock. This old problem is seen, somewhat ironically, in modern church-growth strategies. Outreach becomes the exclusive work of the church, neglecting other essential ministries such as prayer, discipleship, and visitation of the sick. The church becomes no more than an outpost for witness rather than a gospel-centered community. The worship service is watered down in order to be sensitive to potential visitors, who, to be quite honest, would benefit more *in the long run* by witnessing what Christians actually believe and practice rather than a dumbed-down version.

What this often leads to is weak churches that lack deep worship and genuine fellowship. This will hurt outreach, as new believers grow beyond what the church is able to offer them. In more extreme cases, the church built on slick programming rather than discipleship implodes with moral failures. It's a narrative I have witnessed more often than I care to share, even in my own community. Marketing the church is to start off on the wrong foot, yet even marketers know full well, if you have no quality control, eventually the consumer will wise up to the mediocrity of your product. "Even the best admen will admit that, over the long term, all the marketing in the world won't matter if the product hasn't been made right," marketing expert Ryan Holiday admits.[4] A poor product is a poor product, no matter how hard you try to sell it.

One would be hard-pressed not to see this in the American church where a consumer mentality has cheapened the cost of discipleship. A dechurched Christianity is a direct result of putting little to no work into Christian discipleship and all our effort into outreach. As the late J. I. Packer once claimed, "Christianity in America is 3,000 miles wide and half an inch deep."[5] The parish needs to be able to look in and see what kind of Christian life we are offering. If the church is doing what it is supposed to be doing, it basically markets itself. If anything, Christian love is our marketing strategy.

Our (Not So) Secret Weapon

"By this all people will know that you are my disciples," Jesus said, "if you have love for one another" (John 13:35). The reference here is not primarily our love for nonbelievers (however important that is), but Christian love for one another. Our love as a church is our not-so-secret weapon to witness to the world about Jesus Christ. The local church, far from an obstacle to evangelism, is the God-ordained means to share the gospel with the world.

Among the highest factors given as a reason for dechurching was a lack of love from church people or a lack of fitting in.[6]

---

4. Holiday, *Perennial Seller*, 18.

5. Packer, "Future of Evangelicalism?," para. 8.

6. Speaking of the dechurched evangelicals in particular, "when we focused on why this group of people left the church and how they thought they would come back, the answer was simple: belonging." Davis and Graham, *Great Dechurching*, 28.

Many have tried to argue that the church only gets in the way of evangelism or outreach. The idea that our witness would be better off without the church is not only unbiblical but also patently false. Our best tool for outreach is an invitation to a loving, caring, kindhearted community of redeemed believers. Without neglecting the call to go and tell it on the mountain, we need to remember the strategy, "come and you will see" (John 1:38). Put simply, if you are serious about evangelism, you should be serious about churching.

New Englanders are known for being cold towards outsiders. Much of the country might even consider us rude for our apparent lack of hospitality. In my own neighborhood, I still have neighbors who don't wave back to me! In reality, it is a difference of values. New Englanders tend to value efficiency and a close network of friends over casual conversations and a large social circle. However, I have seen more than a few natives thaw out in the context of the church community. A smiling greeter at the door, clear signage and clean restrooms, a warm welcome to any visitors from the pulpit, and most importantly a church congregation that is evidently happy to see new people, go a long way. One recent church member told me, "If we can just get people in the door, we've got them!"

There is a bit of a goldilocks principle here. We have all witnessed overly zealous church members come on too strong. A lot of hugging and touching does not suit most Bostonians. Grabbing newcomers by the arms and dragging them to meet the preacher, as one member once did, is not a good strategy! The look on their faces made it easy to predict they would not be coming back, which they did not. Yet, overall, I find sharing the gospel in the context of a loving church family the most effective evangelistic approach available here among the frozen chosen. It says without words: look around you, the gospel really works. The proof is in the pudding.

A Party in a Parish

Christ is neither against culture nor merely in it. He is using the church to transform the culture. We are a party that transforms a parish, at a pace of one person at a time. The word party has a couple of meanings. One definition is a distinct group of people, distinguished from the crowd. We use the term, for example, in restaurants and fishing trips. A party of five is a bit cumbersome for a private fishing party. The other definition is a celebration, as in a birthday party or party for retirement.

The church-as-party works in both senses of the word. Located in a city or town is a distinct group of people who believe the gospel and have joined a Christian assembly. God has set apart a people for himself to proclaim the excellencies of him who called them out of darkness into his marvelous light (see 1 Pet 2:9–12). As sojourners and exiles we are the gospel party. In the second sense of the word, the church is a perpetual festival celebrating the good news of Jesus. With so many prodigals come home, "it [is] fitting to celebrate and be glad" (Luke 15:32). Let's party! Your community needs to overhear the "music and dancing" (Luke 15:25) of prodigals and know they are welcome here.

This is one of a myriad of reasons why it is important for Christians to be part of a local church. Our faithful presence in the culture is amplified exponentially by how we act while we are together. Do we model Christian love? It is one thing to claim to love God whom we cannot see; it is quite another to love our brother whom we can see (1 John 4:20). The church is our opportunity to demonstrate true love to a skeptical world.

Let me explain practically. For the people of my city to see the bond of Christian love in real time, they must see it through the church. When neighbors watch a disabled member living alone welcomed to Thanksgiving dinner by a family with kids, they witness something of the love of God. When they observe an old man in the hospital visited by a host of church members of all ages, nurses take note of what Christian love looks like. When wealthier members go out of their way to provide Christmas gifts to families in the church who have very little, the neighborhood hears that Christians mean business when it comes to love.

There is no doubt that the church has often spread more heat than light, more anger with the culture than Christian love. What can I say? I've been frustrated with the church as much as the next church member. Yet there is no doubt that my Christian witness has been enhanced immeasurably by my church family.

The Beacons Are Lit

Christian love shines the light of Christ to the parish, and it also acts as a beacon to guide people to join the festivities. The "you" in "you are the light of the world" (Matt 5:14; and in "you are the salt of the earth," Matt 5:13) is plural for a reason. We shine the light together. It is why Jesus can so easily extend the light metaphor to "a city on a hill" (Matt 5:14). It is our corporate witness that shines brightest. However, it is not just a matter of shining the light of Christian love so people can observe it; it is a welcome signal. Like a lighthouse, it calls people to *terra firma*.

To tweak the nautical analogy a bit, the church sounds the call to enter the ark and find refuge. "If anyone could escape who was outside the ark of Noah," Cyprian challenged, "then he also may escape who shall be outside of the Church."[7] If those in the community come to faith in Jesus, where will they gather to worship? Where will they go to grow in grace? Where will they learn how to join the mission? The answer biblically is as obvious as a boat on top of Mount Ararat. Have them come and join the party!

Christian love starts with the church but always flows outward into the parish and the world. Anyone who believes Christian love is meant only for the church family has misunderstood how Christian love works. It cannot help but spill out into the streets. Jesus made clear that our love for one another extends to love for our neighbor and even love for our enemies. When the world sees the love within a church community also extended to the kid who vandalized the church doors by welcoming him to church, a recognizable light is shone. When the woman who maligned the church on social media falls on challenging times and the church helps her with her bills, the light flickers a little brighter. Christian love is not motivated by showing off, but it is also not meant to be put

---

7. Cyprian, *Unity of the Church*, para. 6.

under a bushel. "Let your light shine before others, so that they may see your good works and give glory to your Father who is in heaven" (Matt 5:16).

The Early Church

The reason why the church was able to reach the known world so quickly was primarily through the shocking nature of Christian love. In a mostly barbaric world, Christian love stood out like a torch in a dungeon. The early church had a message and a lifestyle shaped by that message that was irresistible to the Roman Empire. It wouldn't be too long before the Emperor Constantine himself bowed the knee to Jesus Christ. Consider these characteristics afresh that the early church held to so dearly.

They supported the poor. This should be no surprise, as both Jesus and the entire New Testament call us to do this. What is particularly remarkable is how the early Christians took care of even their enemies' poor. Julian the Apostate (ruled 361–63), who wished to restore paganism to the Roman Empire, had to admit, "It is disgraceful that, when no Jew ever has to beg, and the impious Galilaeans [Christians] support not only their own poor but ours as well, all men see that our people lack aid from us."[8] Generosity to their poor was a tangible way to love their enemies.

They cared for the sick. Plagues have wreaked havoc on human history, and in each case since the resurrection, Christians have used them as times to shine the light of Christ. Eusebius, the church historian, described their actions during the plague:

> Heedless of danger, they took charge of the sick, attending to their every need and ministering to them in Christ, and with them departed this life serenely happy; for they were infected by others with the disease, drawing on themselves the sickness of their neighbors and cheerfully accepting their pains. Many, in nursing and

---

8. Julian the Apostate, *Letters*, para. 22.

curing others, transferred their death to themselves and died in their stead.[9]

He goes on to compare Christian love with the fear and indifference of their heathen neighbors:

> But with the heathen everything was quite otherwise. They deserted those who began to be sick, and fled from their dearest friends. They shunned any participation or fellowship with death; which yet, with all their precautions, it was not easy for them to escape.[10]

Plagues, natural disasters, and times of war have been seasons when churches had opportunity to step up and display Christian love. On a small scale, during COVID-19, churches in my city actively sought to minister to the vulnerable elderly, offer food to the disenfranchised, and drop off meals for those who were quarantined. It was a proud moment for the church.

They adopted the unwanted. Infanticide has been its own sort of plague throughout human history. Oftentimes to avoid expensive dowries, people would abandon female babies to the streets. Christians took this opportunity to adopt these children as their very own. Augustine testifies,

> Again, sometimes foundlings which heartless parents have exposed in order to their being cared for [*sic*.] by any passer-by, are picked up by holy virgins, and are presented for baptism by these persons, who neither have nor desire to have children of their own.[11]

It wasn't until 374 that Valentinian I, a Christian emperor of Rome, made killing an infant a form of homicide. This practice continued however, as did adopting these unwanted babies, as one historian notes.

> That is about the year 787, an arch-priest named Datheus, established at Milan, at his own expense, a foundling

---

9. Eusebius, *History of the Church*, 7.22.
10. Eusebius, *History of the Church*, 10.22.
11. Augustine, "Letter 98," para. 6.

> hospital, in order to put a stop to the crime of child-murder.... With this view he purchased a house near the church, and issued an order that the foundlings should be suckled in it by hired nurses, and educated for seven years. They were to be taught some handicraft; to be supplied in the establishment with food, clothing and shoes, and at the age of seven to be discharged as free-born.[12]

Still today, Christians lead the way in foster care and adoptions.

They practiced equality and unity. Church historian Michael Green describes the radical love of the Christian faith in Rome, leveling the spiritual field between all people:

> But materially there was a difference—in the quality of the fellowship. Here were societies in which aristocrats and slaves, Roman citizens and provincials, rich and poor mixed on equal terms and without distinction: societies which possessed a quality of caring and love which was unique. Herein lay its attraction.[13]

This was so shocking enemies of the Christian faith used it as a weapon to mock the early church: "They manifestly show that they desire and are able to gain over only the silly, and the mean, and the stupid, with women and children."[14] What Celsus meant as an insult, Christians upheld as a badge of honor.

The early church practiced Christian love, a love that stood out to the world around them. The world mostly knew a humanity determined by hierarchy and merit, scorning the downtrodden and weak. Historian Tom Holland describes the world the early church shone light into:

> The heroes of the *Iliad*, favourites of the gods, golden and predatory, had scorned the weak and downtrodden. So too, for all the honour that Julian paid them, had philosophers. The starving deserved no sympathy. Beggars were best rounded up and deported. Pity risked undermining a wise man's self-control. Only fellow citizens of

---

12. Beckmann, *History of Inventions*, 1341.
13. Green, *Evangelism and the Early Church*, 255.
14. Origen, *Contra Celsum*, ch. 44.

good character who, through no fault of their own, had fallen on evil days might conceivably merit assistance.[15]

While there is a danger in romanticizing the early church too much, there is no doubt that Christian love, self-sacrificial and indiscriminate, was something the world had yet to witness. When the world takes notice, they give ear to the only message that can save and transform, the gospel of Jesus Christ.

Mission Drift

The mission of the church has been heartily debated.[16] I don't want to rehash old arguments but to say the church cannot save the world. Individual Christians may have individual vocations to engage in politics, social services, and international affairs worldwide. Christians often make up a lion's share of the military, Congress, and America's voting block, and for good reasons. However, few I think would want a particular church, no matter how savvy its members, waging war, rewriting the Constitution, or overseeing child protective services. Let individual disciples go out and be wise servants in the world. Let the church make disciples and then equip these disciples to, with biblical principles and a gospel mission, point people to Jesus as the ultimate good.

It is easy to drift into dangerous eddies. I asked an influential Brazilian pastor what he thinks of the current state of the church in Brazil. While overall he is impressed, he warned that many have become too involved in politics. It has already begun to stunt the church's growth, both spiritually and numerically. The issue here in the United States is at least equally as bad. Like a dog chasing after one squirrel and then another, we are so easily distracted by issues that, though worthy of attention, lead us off course and oftentimes into shipwreck. What we so easily miss is that the best

---

15. Holland, *Dominion*, 10.

16. For a good balanced book on this subject, consider DeYoung and Gilbert, *What Is the Mission of the Church?*

way to challenge many of these political ills in the long run is to stay focused on the gospel itself.

If I might be so bold as to offer a controversial example. I am pro-life. That is probably no surprise coming from a Christian pastor. But I would rather spend my time counseling and caring for pregnant moms and supporting our local Pregnancy Care Center than lobbying legislators. Abortion laws are written by people and voted on by constituents whose hearts are either tender to the unborn made in the *imago Dei* or not. Winning the laws for one generation may end up a pyrrhic victory if the next generation is enraged to fight back with a fury. But if the church spends its time seeking to change hearts, we may ensure a pro-life future and, in the end, save countless more lives.

Wise Counsel

Think about how your church is influencing your parish. Consider ways you could be involved in serving the community. If there is not a ministry serving the city or town, start some conversations about what a meaningful ministry for your church context would look like. Think about inviting some friends and neighbors in the community to go to church services so they can see the church in action. Welcome visitors warmly to your gatherings so they can see Christian love in the context of Christian community.

Discussion Questions

1. Describe your parish. What characteristics define the community around your church family? What type of struggles do people in your city or town struggle with? What activities do they love to do?
2. What ministries does your church have to serve people outside the church family? How could these ministries be more effective? What new ministries do you think the church should consider to better serve?

3. Is the way your church treats one another an example of Christian love? How might your church's love for one another become part of their witness for the city to see? Do you ever invite people to church?

4. Are there areas your church has drifted from the mission? How has that negatively affected the church's witness in the community? In what ways could the church narrow its focus for a better witness?

7

The Church Is the Mission

PLANT AND REVITALIZE

When people hear that I am Korean, a follow-up question is sometimes, "North or South?" I don't mind the question, but it is a funny one when you understand the statistics. You would be very hard-pressed to find a North Korean in the United States. You are about as likely to meet an astronaut as a North Korean immigrant in America. South Koreans on the other hand have immigrated throughout North America in large numbers in every American city.

The story of Christian mission to the Korean peninsula is remarkable. In the year 1900, only about 1 percent of South Koreans would identify themselves as Christians. According to Pew Research, three in ten consider themselves Christians today.[1] Churches populate every city from Seoul to Gunsan (where my mother is from). Korea even boasts the largest congregation in the world, Yoido Full Gospel Church. Sometimes called the Korean Pentecost, the explosion of Christianity in South Korea has been witnessed by a watching world over the last century and a half.

As the story goes, the gospel came to the Hermit Kingdom by a Welshman named Robert Thomas, who boarded the SS General Sherman in September 1865. Upon arrival, the ship was attacked

---

1. Connor, "South Korea's Population," 2.

by the Koreans and then responded with gunfire, killing several of the natives. During the attack, Thomas kept yelling the Korean word for peace but to no avail. The vessel was set to fire by the Koreans, and the crew and Thomas abandoned ship and reached the shore. The missionary handed out as many Bibles as he could before he was stabbed to death, minutes after setting his feet on dry land. One Bible reached Park Young-sik who wallpapered his guesthouse with it. After reading the pages of the Bible, he came to faith. Years later, people would come from all over the kingdom to read the words decorating the guesthouse, many coming to faith. These believers would plant Nuldarigol Chapel, the first Christian church in Pyongyang.

Today the peninsula is divided by the demilitarized zone (DMZ), a 2.5-mile-thick border, and just north of the DMZ, lies North Korea. The number of Christians in the Democratic People's Republic of Korea is unknown, as are many statistics about the country under an oppressive dictatorship. By most accounts, it is less than 2 percent; and the number of recognized, state-approved Christian churches? Four.[2]

The penalty for professing an unauthorized faith in North Korea, let alone leading an underground house church, is imprisonment that will often lead to death. Thousands of North Korean Christians are in prison camps and are beaten and even killed by prison guards with no consequence. It remains a closed off country that will take extraordinary sacrifices to reach with the gospel.

The Gospel Not Known

The missionary strategy of the New Testament was simple, albeit dangerous. Go preach the gospel in the synagogue and then the marketplace (Gr. *agora*) until some people come to faith. Then start meeting with converts for a while to start up a church in the pagan city. When the time is right, leave them behind to the work

---

2. US Department of State, "2020 Report," sec. 2.

of the Holy Spirit and check on them by epistle or by a return visit. Repeat the process throughout the Roman Empire.

What is clear from the New Testament is that the church played a vital role in the Great Commission. The goal was not to make isolated converts throughout Asia Minor. It was to create communities of faith that would mature together. The Christians would reach their neighbors, the church would grow numerically, elders would emerge, and eventually they would send out missionaries of their own to reach the empire and beyond.

If you were to remove the church from this process, you would end up with confused individuals trying to figure out how to live the Christian life with no clear direction—no shepherds, no corporate worship, and no fellowship. Surely the Great Commission would have faltered. Like the dechurched West, Christianity would have begun to blunder into subjectivism. Christians would have splintered into sects and syncretism and would not have lasted beyond a single generation.

This is not to remove the role of the Holy Spirit in missions. The book of Acts shows us a radical dependence on the work of the Spirit. No one would have come to faith to begin with if the Spirit were not at work. The Spirit calls missionaries. It is the Lord who makes a way; as with the first missionaries, "he had opened a door of faith to the Gentiles" (Acts 14:27). He also closes doors by his Spirit—for example, "having been forbidden by the Holy Spirit to speak the word in Asia" (Acts 16:6) and "when they had come up to Mysia, they attempted to go into Bithynia, but the Spirit of Jesus did not allow them" (Acts 16:6–7). What is more, the missionaries would never be willing to leave a local church behind, trusting that when returning it would have matured, if they did not believe the Holy Spirit was at work guiding and protecting them.

It is to say, however, that their understanding of how the Spirit works towards the sanctification of new Christians was inextricably tied to their local church. He grants the church spiritual gifts (Gr. *charismata*) to be used to build up the body of Christ, as "each is given the manifestation of the Spirit for the common good" (1 Cor 12:7). He raises up shepherds to care for the church till it matures to "manhood" (Eph 4:11–16). To ignore the centrality of the church would be to ignore the means of grace God has granted to accomplish the Great Commission.

If we are going to reach the 10/40 Window, the primary target of global missions, we are going to need to plant a lot of churches. The Joshua Project defines the 10/40 Window as "the rectangular area of North Africa, the Middle East and Asia, approximately between 10 degrees north and 40 degrees north latitude," which "includes the majority of the world's Muslims, Hindus, and Buddhists."[3] There are not enough missionaries on the planet, or even throughout history, to reach the billions yet to hear the name Jesus. But thousands of native churches within these ethnic groups? That is not only comprehendible but also profoundly biblical.

Colonialism?

Personally, I think the boogeyman of Western colonialism has been exaggerated. That said, there are pitfalls that global missions have fallen into over the centuries. Merchants have found missions expedient for their own financial ends. Missionaries have too often confused evangelism with imposing Western customs. American and European dress, hymns, and norms have been imposed as the only way Christianity can exist. There has been a fear that missions will swallow up beautiful foreign cultures, which will then be lost forever.

Most missionaries today are very mindful of these pitfalls and are far more nuanced and savvier than people realize. We have come a long way. Their desire is to bring the gospel into a culture to redeem lives within it. Most missionaries I know demonstrate a deep respect and love for the culture they are serving in, and the last thing in the world they would want is to destroy that culture. They have spent years learning the language, studying the norms,

---

3. Joshua Project, "What Is the 10/40 Window?," para. 1.

and getting to know their people group. I need to remind them that Western culture is great too, you know!

One of the easiest ways to protect against colonialism is to ensure natives are leading their own churches. The goal is not to create churches that remain dependent on the teaching, resources, and leadership of foreign missionaries. The goal is to raise up native churches that the missionaries can eventually leave behind to the work of the Holy Spirit. The best way to do this is to help plant churches that function in a biblical way and to work yourself out of a job. The best missionaries know this well: our job is to replace our job with a mature native Christian leader or leaders.

Going back to Nepal, one of the observations I had with Christian churches was that they were singing mostly Nepali tunes and dressed in traditional Nepali attire (they even give their guests colorful Nepali hats as a sign of hospitality). More than that, they engaged in Nepali dances in their worship. This was no colonialism; it was the fruition of a beautiful culture being ushered into worship of the true and living God!

Church Revitalization

Much of the world has been Christianized already. Abandoned church buildings tell the story. Cathedrals are the ghost of Christianity past. Over the centuries, Christianity has waxed and waned, and in Europe it's done more waning than waxing. Europe is leading the way in a post-Christian dechurched culture.

My South Korean mother married my Irish American father. The history of Irish Christianity is much different than that of the Korean peninsula. For one, it is much older. Celtic Christianity dates to AD 400 with the missionary work of St. Patrick. Ireland was untouched by the Protestant Reformation of the 1500s and remained staunchly Roman Catholic. However, as of late, this commitment to the Church of Rome has begun to drastically change. More so than in the United States, the Irish are leaving the church in droves. Statistics paint a dreary picture. In 1975, weekly church attendance in the Emerald Isle was 91 percent, and in 2020 it dropped to 27 percent. No doubt it is even worse post-COVID. That is dechurching at its most extreme.

I am writing this on a plane home to Boston from Dublin, after spending some time with conservative evangelical pastors and churches in the west of Ireland. Ireland is undoubtedly beautiful, with its rolling fields of various shades of green, dotted with white sheep and punctuated with old stone buildings. What particularly struck me were the Celtic cross headstones lining the small-town cemeteries. They speak of a long and rich history of Christian devotion and sacrifice. But these crosses represent the dead, a rich Christian past replaced by a vague and aimless secularism. The good news is Jesus Christ specializes in resurrections.

What is needed is a lot more than church planting. We also need to revitalize churches that have lost the mission. The mission field is no longer the global south and east, it is now the *globe*, period. In many ways, churches in Africa, Asia, and South America are doing better than those in much of the West. Many churches from these continents have begun to send missionaries to North America and Europe, hoping to revitalize the land that originally sent them missionaries. Even if not intentionally sent as missionaries, they are coming as immigrants who bring their strong Christian faith with them. They join churches, or start new ones, that work towards the revitalization and replacement of dying ones.

We cannot afford to ignore the dechurching in North America, Europe, and Australia when it comes to missions. Mission boards have begun to see these countries as veritable mission fields, and thankfully so. It may not seem like quite the same sacrifice to go and serve in Luxembourg, but luxury is no indicator of spiritual wealth.[4] One might argue that missions in European and North American cities is more strategic than anywhere else. If we lose the historic missionary sending countries, who also still give the bulk of missionary funding, we lose far more eventually. Even if one chooses not to see the Great Commission in such an

---

4. Personally, I have found Luxembourg to be one of the most beautiful countries I have visited. It was so magical my daughter told me she doesn't like to think about our time there as it makes her sad that we are not there!

analytic way, these cities are populated with more non-Christians than many south of the equator.

The good news is that in virtually all these cities and towns, there is a long history of Christian faith. We are not starting from scratch. There are church buildings readily available. There are Bibles long translated into their native languages. The groundwork of Christianity is already laid. The church is ready to be revitalized if we would just get to it. Pray without ceasing, love your neighbors, share the gospel, and invite people to church.

Average Joe and Ordinary Jane

If you had to guess, would you wager that the gospel spread primarily via trained clergy or by lay people sharing their faith with their neighbors? If you guessed the laity, you would be correct. Michael Green reveals, "Christianity was from its inception a lay movement, and so it continued for a remarkably long time."[5] Similarly, prominent church historian Adolf von Harnack writes, "We cannot hesitate to believe that the great mission of Christianity was in reality accomplished by means of informal missionaries."[6] It is the average Joe and ordinary Jane church member who were the primary unit for reaching the ancient world. In Christ, we become anything but average and ordinary. We become literal world changers.

This is not a dig at seminaries or Bible colleges, which have played a necessary role in the Great Commission. I am a grateful product of them. It is tragic to watch the steep decline in enrollment in most of them. Anecdotally, there is a Bible college in my own city that has struggled to maintain a critical mass of students since its move here less than twenty years ago, even with a campus entirely gifted to them! Even if this trend were to turn around, at best these institutions can only train a small percentage of what is realistically needed to reach the nations. Add to this the fact that

---

5. Green, *Evangelism in the Early Church*, 243.
6. Harnack, *Early Christianity*, 368.

many countries will balk at a seminary trained missionary entering their borders. Mechanics, nurses, and engineers have access to many countries like, say, Senegal or Iran—places professional missionaries or ordained clergy may never see.

This trend puts even more responsibility on local churches to make sure they are discipling their members well. If sending off members to expensive theological institutes is not a possibility, local churches can themselves be the training ground for faithful Christian ministry and for prepping people for global missions. If a single local church feels unequipped to train leaders in various subjects (e.g., New Testament Greek or missiology), mentors can be shared across local churches if needed, and the number of useful resources available online has never been more accessible. Short-term mission trips provide indispensable real-world experience on how to do missions for the long term, if so called. If someone is unready and unequipped to do ministry in their home church, there is no reason to think they will be suddenly equipped and ready to do so on the mission field. What better place to learn how to do ministry than in the context of a local church, which is itself the multiplying unit for Great Commission expansion?

In the global community we find ourselves in, the door for equipped lay people to work around the world and plug into a church while living abroad is wide open. Your part of the Great Commission may be as simple as living in a country that needs revitalization, finding a good church, and in time inviting your neighbors.

New England Missions

I am a native New Englander. We are proud of our heritage and rich American history. We have the best colleges in the country, the best hospitals and doctors in the world, and the best sports teams in the league! At least that is what we believe. The six states of New England, with our autumn leaves and colonial homes, are iconic Americana in my mind.

CHURCHING

What happens in New England often acts as a harbinger for what will happen in the rest of the United States, due in large part to the influence of the universities. What has happened in New England is advanced dechurching. The Roman Catholic child abuse scandal sped up a process that was already in place. Evangelical Christianity is the lowest in the country, with percentages in the low single digits. A Bible believing Christian in Massachusetts or Maine is an odd mallard. New England is often recognized as the only mission field in the United States.

That said, there does appear to be hope on the horizon. This subtle growth is still too nascent to be sure. Vermont, often considered the nation's most secular state, has experienced what some have called a silent revival, doubling the number of evangelicals in the last decade.[7] Within my own denomination, the Baptist Churches of New England was the only network in the Southern Baptist world that saw growth rather than decline.[8] Much of this is due to an embrace of ethnic congregations, such as Brazilian and Haitian churches, that other parts of the country have been slow to incorporate.

The growth has been coupled with a commitment to the local church. Take for example, the newly founded ministry Small Town Summits, which serves the hundreds of small towns dotting the landscape of the northeast. Its goal is not merely personal pietism but is tied inextricably to the gospel and the local church: "to see the small places of New England filled with gospel-centered, community-engaged churches and Christian workers, for the glory of God."[9] It is too early to tell, but New England may just lead the way in a robust, ecclesiological revitalization.

In my own city of Haverhill, Massachusetts, this has been undeniable. Many pulpits in the city once pastored by mainline or liberal clergy are now filled by evangelicals. Several new churches have been planted in the old colonial town, established in 1640.

---

7. Page, "Evangelicals Doubled in Last Decade."

8. Roach, "Southern Baptists Crack 'Yankee Stoicism.'"

9. For a comprehensive understanding of the ministry of Small Town Summits, see Witmer, *Big Gospel*.

The Brazilian congregation that shares space with my church is one of the largest Portuguese-speaking churches in Massachusetts and experienced all their growth in the last five years. I can remember growing up, K–12, in Haverhill public schools and hardly finding a single friend who took their Christian faith seriously. That would not be the experience of a Christian teenager in the city today. It is too early to tell, but I am hopeful we have reached a dechurched bottoming out before the rest of the country and have begun to rise in a way that takes churching seriously.

If this is the direction of the country, and even the West, we may be in for some "times of refreshing" (Acts 3:20).

Wise Counsel

Pray about your role in missions. Every Christian should be involved in the Great Commission, even if that means no more than committing to your local church, giving faithfully in support of missionaries, and praying regularly for the gospel to reach the nations. Be open to the possibility that God would have you do more. Are you open to living abroad, intentionally looking to go to a country in need of greater Christian witness? This may mean going somewhere within the 10/40 Window, or it may mean serving in a church in Europe and reaching out to your neighbors. Let the Holy Spirit lead you, even as you seek wise counsel from Christian leaders you respect.

Discussion Questions

1. What has been your experience with missions? Have you spent time on the mission field or with missionaries? What has your impression of them been? Did they show respect to foreign cultures and people?
2. Describe the role of the church in missions in the New Testament. What might the advantage be for people who come

to faith to be part of their own native church? What pitfalls would this approach avoid?

3. How has your own church played a role in the Great Commission? Do you know the names of the missionaries your church supports? Do you keep up with what is going on in their lives and in their ministry? How could you do better at this?

4. Do you think God might use you to serve in missions, at least for a portion of your life? If not in the 10/40 Window, how might he use you to serve in a post-Christian context, such as somewhere in western Europe?

8

The Good Rechurching

WHERE DO WE GO FROM HERE?

I PLANNED MY SABBATICAL to a tee. I had been senior pastor at the church for ten years, on staff for sixteen years. I was blessed to receive a generous grant from Lilly Endowment to be used for "clergy renewal." With the full support of my church family, I detailed the three-month break carefully. For the first segment, I would travel from New England to old England to tour the British Isles. Then I would spend some time hanging out in one of the greatest cities on earth, a segment I called "Life in London." With an apartment all set up, I would commute outward to places like The Eagle and Child (the pub where C. S. Lewis and J. R. R. Tolkien often met). For the third segment, I would fly to the Dominican Republic and enjoy some rest and relaxation with the family. It was going to be something! It was all planned out for the summer of 2020. Then the world shut down.

I was able to do none of what was planned that year as international travel gave way to a global pandemic.[1] Instead, I spent the sabbatical almost entirely stateside. (We did get to end our trip with two weeks in Mexico!) We visited parts of the United States I had never been to: South Dakota, Wyoming, and Montana. It was

---

1. I was grateful to spend time traveling around the British Isles in 2024, but 2020 travel from the United States to most of Europe was prohibited.

not what was planned, but in the end, it was perfect. Anyone from cowboy country, or at least familiar with the region, will know what I mean when I say it was rejuvenating. The natural beauty, the friendly but not imposing hospitality, and the big nighttime sky were the perfect recipe for rest and renewal. Yellowstone's Grand Prismatic Spring and the Grand Teton Mountain range, along with endless elk and bison sightings, were not on the original to-see list, but were a surprise twist I will treasure so long as I have a memory that can remember.

If the goal of a sabbatical is to refresh, Jackson Hole was medicine for the soul. Grabbing a cup of coffee in the crisp morning summer air, sitting in front of a fire with the mountains in view, has now become my defining picture for rest. In hindsight, I would not change a thing. It wasn't the plan I laid out, but it was the Lord's will. "Many are the plans in the mind of a man, but it is the purpose of the Lord that will stand" (Prov 19:21).

Out of Vogue

The American church has been addicted to the faddish, the avant-garde, and the new for too long. We are searching for that new book from some new dynamic author that will be the key to spiritual renewal. Pastors latch on to a new church growth resource with a new methodology that will be the silver bullet for ministry. Laymen want spiritual renewal based on some new concept from a new self-help guru. A bestseller, a popular podcast, or a killer evangelistic strategy will be the answer we have all been seeking.

What if the answer was right under our noses all along? What if the answer is the ordinary strategy of getting back to churching—that is, commitment and service to a local church? It may not be very sexy, but it is tried and true. If dechurching has starved us with spiritual malnourishment, it may be time to go back to where we know there is plenty of food.

If you are heading down the wrong path, the quickest way to right it is to stop in your tracks and head back to the fork where things went wrong. To keep going forward is to go further away from your destination. Not that our desire should be to turn back the clock entirely. Much good has happened in the last twenty-five years. New missionaries have gone out, bad pastors have been exposed, and we made it through a horrible pandemic. I for one have no desire to relive all that.

We cannot revive the past even if we wanted to, which we do not. There is no making the church great again via nostalgia for a bygone era. The problem with bygone eras is, first, that they have gone by, but next, they were not as great as we imagine they were. We tend to whitewash the muckiness of the past, remembering only what was good and conveniently ignoring what was bad. And much of the past was ugly.

There is a reason the past twenty-five-years or so led to dechurching and not revival. The remedy of abandoning the church was a poor one, but it was not born out of a complete misdiagnosis. The church has been sick for a time. Before we jump into rechurching, it might be wise to consider the maladies of the past in hopes that a rechurched future would be far healthier. Churching done right would mean learning from the mistakes of our predecessors, and maturing past them, to be reformed and always reforming according to the word of God.

Churching Reimagined

If I had a magic wand and could reinvent how we do churching, there are several things I would wish we would do better. Here are a handful.

We desperately need a renewed emphasis on prayer. Few would disagree with the call to pray, but it needs to go beyond the trite and cliché. We need to start praying together in our churches. This should have been a bare minimum, but it often was not. It is certainly the case that a lack of prayer prefaced a move to dechurching. Put positively, a church that prays together would be far less likely to lose members who value the blessings that come with prayer. Methods and strategies are easy to disagree about, but prayer has a bonding effect that goes beyond the psychological or intellectual. We might have had megachurch buildings, conferences that would descend on major cities and bring in high-caliber speakers, and high-tech multimedia ministries, but did we pray? Prayer is a spiritual work. More than I value a church that is well-oiled and organized, I will take a church that pleads with God. At the very least they are doing what Christians should be doing "without ceasing" (1 Thess 5:17).

Next, we need churching that takes seriously care for the poor. The ongoing fights about social justice and neo-Marxism at some point become merely academic. The person arguing for theological purity and deathly afraid the church will slide into liberalism if we talk too much about alleviating poverty is missing a basic Christian principle: love thy neighbor. At some point, a wiser elder statesman of the church should say, why don't we just ignore all this social justice bunk and start helping the people in our city who need a jacket for the winter? Of course, we want to tell them about Jesus as we help them, but it would be a loving thing to do to make sure they are not hungry and cold when we do so.

That some churches have lost the gospel along the road of social action should not paralyze us to do what should have been instinctual for churches to be doing. A church does not have to be fluent in critical theory to understand helping the poor in their city is not the end-all for a Christian community. It is, however, basic Christian decency: "Only, they asked us to remember the poor, the very thing I was eager to do" (Gal 2:10).

Third, and most importantly, we need to get back to teaching the Bible. Biblical literacy is comically low among Christians. According to Lifeway Research, only two in five churchgoers knew that the Roman mythology of Remus and Romulus was not in the Bible.[2] The expectation that church is where you learn the Bible was at one point assumed. Movie clips, impressive PowerPoint presentations, and tear-jerking stories aside, do the people attending church services understand the Bible more having attended?

Do they know biblical theology culminates in the person and work of Jesus Christ? Do they understand the *imago Dei*, the

2. Earls, "Overconfident," para. 11.

theology of penal substitutionary atonement, and the Christian hope of the resurrection, not as independent doctrines of Christianity but within the very flow of the Scriptural narrative? Churching needs to get back to the church as a barracks that equips people to know what the Bible says and how to read it. Preachers are not celebrities or mere motivational speakers but people of the good book, both in teaching and in lifestyle.[3] If I could reimagine churching, pastors would get back to clearly, simply, consistently teaching the Bible. People would know, "If I want to learn the Bible, I go to church."

I Challenge You to Do Better

The race issue in America has played a significant role in dechurching. The way the church developed into ethnically distinct congregations is strange to the New Testament, even if all too familiar today. Chinese churches, Haitian congregations, African, Anglo, and whatever other varieties we find is a development foreign to the New Testament model, where "there is not Greek and Jew, circumcised and uncircumcised, barbarian, Scythian, slave, free; but Christ is all, and in all" (Col 3:11).

Integrating is a difficult task, for sure. How do we take into consideration cultural differences, some of which we do not want to lose? Can we incorporate rich Puritan hymns and African spirituals? Even harder, language is a barrier. Anyone who has sat through interpreted sermons knows it is not ideal for weekly worship. These are not easy issues to resolve, and I do not pretend to have the answers. I am happy to lay the challenge to the next generation to do better. If you can find a way to reengage churching by overcoming the obstacles of race and ethnic differences that previous generations have overwhelmingly failed to overcome, what an improvement that would be.

---

3. Os Guinness explains the puzzling response of a Japanese businessman talking to an Australian: "Whenever I meet a Buddhist leader, I meet a holy man. Whenever I meet a Christian leader, I meet a manager." Guinness, *Dining with the Devil*, 49.

Dechurching due to political differences is another major factor. We are divided more by politics than ethnicity (often the political line is drawn closer to racial or ethnic lines than we care to admit). Ex-vangelicals, those who formally identified as evangelicals, list politics among the top reasons for dechurching.[4] The vitriol the political angst in the United States has produced, so often infiltrating the church, speaks for itself. Again, there are no easy answers.

While some churches have come down hard on one side of the aisle or the other, equating Christian faith with partisan issues or even candidates, others choose to ignore politics altogether, seeing it as taboo in the church. I am not sure if a complete expulsion of all things political is the right approach (e.g., certainly abolitionism seemed a worthy church topic in the nineteenth century), but it has been at least preferable to nationalism on one side or the constant capitulation to Marxist ideals on the other. I will say that in a country as divided as we are, there is something to say about Christians who radically disagree on, say, economic policies or government intervention, who are able to sit at a table together and enjoy a meal. Once again, I challenge a rechurching generation to do better. I do not have the perfect answer, nor do I imagine there is one. I will join you as you work to improve the church and find better solutions. Consider the torch passed.

For King and Country

It is one of the kingdom's great ironies that an unwavering focus on heaven causes Christians to do the most good in this world. Christianity transformed the world not because it focused on the here and now but because it could envision a better world. An improved society would be one step closer to the world to come. As C. S. Lewis writes,

> If you read history you will find that the Christians who did most for the present world were just those who

---

4. Davis and Graham, *Great Dechurching*, 74–75.

thought most of the next. The Apostles themselves, who set on foot the conversion of the Roman Empire, the great men who built up the Middle Ages, the English Evangelicals who abolished the Slave Trade, all left their mark on Earth, precisely because their minds were occupied with Heaven.[5]

The good the church does flows from the gospel it believes and its love of heaven.

I once stood in John Newton's pulpit at St. Mary Woolnoth in London. What was most striking to me was the size of the worship space. It was far smaller than I pictured in my head, seating no more than one hundred souls. In this small church building, the wretched ex-slaver preached the gospel of amazing grace to a young William Wilberforce, who led the charge against the slave trade. To take the church out of the equation would have altered the outcome of abolitionism in England, and subsequently in America, in ways we thankfully will never know.

Whereas Marxist ideology puts all its hopes on a social utopia in the here and now, and in doing so has caused little other than pain and division, the church, by setting its sights on an age to come, does true good in this world. To produce the good Christianity has produced takes a vision far bigger than a utopia imagined from rearranging the broken shards of this fallen world. To change the world, Christians have relied on an infinitely good God; as James Davison Hunter puts it, "Any good that is generated by Christians is only the net effect of caring for something more than the good created."[6]

All this to say, if the church ceases to do good in this world, it is a revelation that it has lost its focus on the world to come. Christian hope leads to Christian charity. Rather than a force for division, whether political, cultural, or otherwise, let the church be a force for good in the world. As the church improves society with a vision greater than anything extant in a fallen world, it points

---

5. Lewis, *Complete C. S. Lewis*, 112.
6. Hunter, *To Change the World*, 234.

people to what is to come, "a new heaven and a new earth" (Rev 21:1).

A Bright Future

It seems to me that the church in the West has experienced a chastening. That is not a discouragement to me—quite the opposite. Like a well-deserved scolding, a chastening is meant to bring about positive changes.

The church in the West had it all. We had numerous seminaries with large enrollments. We had megachurches bigger than many small cities. We had incredible wealth flowing through mission organizations and biblical ministries. It is not all gone, not even close. It is drastically changing. Seminaries are hurting, the definition of a megachurch has been reduced, and several ministries have ended. It is hard not to conclude that we squandered it. We peddled it away when we could have nearly reached the world with the gospel had we been wiser. We deserve the spanking we got, and far worse.

Did the spiritual decline cause the dechurching, or did dechurching cause decline? No doubt the downward spiral was the two feeding off each other. This cycle has viciously harmed Christianity. Yet here we are. The spiral may not be finished and there may be far more dechurching to come. However, we are now presented with a unique opportunity to work at churching done rightly. This may not have been the plan we would have mapped out, losing tens of millions of attenders before learning some invaluable lessons, but God's ways and thoughts are higher than ours (see Isa 55:8–9).

What might be most encouraging of all is to know the majority of those who left have admitted they are open to coming back: "51 percent of the dechurched evangelicals we surveyed said they think they *will* one day return to church."[7] While we might think that dechurching means people have hardened themselves against

---

7. Davis and Graham, *Great Dechurching*, 120 (italics original).

the church, the vast majority are open to invitation. "If invited and accompanied," blogs Thom Rainer, "82% of the unchurched are open to attending church with a friend or acquaintance."[8] The solution might be as simple as to start doing churching right and prolifically invite people to church again!

Love the Church

I love the local church. I have dedicated my life to her. I grew up Roman Catholic and have grown to appreciate the foundation I received from the Church of Rome. When I came to fully embrace the gospel of grace, I joined a Baptist church. I went straight from college to seminary and from seminary to pastoral ministry. Since then, I have visited dozens of churches throughout the United States and around the world. Over the years, I have attended churches of nearly every denomination I could find, and many independent and nondenominational churches. I have experienced the ugly underbelly of church life. I could share some horror stories. There have been many days when walking away from the church sounded relieving. Some days it still does! There are church wounds and scars that I will carry to the grave, and I am sure I have caused more than my fair share of hurt to others.

Yet, I still love the church. I owe the church a debt I will never repay. Churching has shown me Jesus Christ more clearly. Without the church, I would not know him as well as I do today. She is his bride and is worth fighting for. I have no doubt that I will be hurt again by the church in the future, many times. That still doesn't dissuade me. There is no way forward that leads anywhere good for Christianity without her. I have not given up on the church and never will. I hope to serve the church until my final breath and then join the church triumphant. Without the slightest hesitation, I encourage you to do the same.

---

8. Rainer, "Solves Most Church Problems," para. 7.

Churching

Wise Counsel

Pray for ways the church can do better going forward. Fight for your church to be better in ways it failed in the past. Don't quit or walk away! Have hard conversations about race with church leaders. Let them know how you feel about politics in the church. Suggest ways you think the church can take care of the poor in the city. If you have proven your commitment to the church, good leaders will want to hear what you have to say. Even if they don't, keep pushing for improvement.

Discussion Questions

1. In what ways do you think the church in the West deserved the dechurching that has happened in the last twenty-five years? In your opinion, what have been its most glaring failures and mistakes?

2. How would you reimagine churching going forward if you had the magic wand to change it? What ways do you think the church could do better going forward? How could the church do better with race and politics specifically?

3. Do you know how to read the Bible better because of your church? What biblical doctrines or theological issues do you think the church needs to teach more about? Why do you think this is needed?

4. Do you love the local church? Why do you think the church is hard for us to love at times? How might you help someone who says, "I love God, and I even read the Bible, but I can't get myself to love the church"?

Conclusion

CHURCHING FOR THE GOSPEL

May we never lose the gospel. My ministry at my church is gospel centered and gospel saturated. I hope to lead people to salvation by personal repentance and faith in Jesus Christ. I then want to shepherd them throughout life to hold firmly to the faith "once for all delivered to the saints" (Jude 3). At the end of their lives, if so privileged, I hope to assist them as they transition into glory holding on to Christ alone by faith alone. And even after death, the funeral is designed to magnify their witness one more time proclaiming the gospel of grace to their family and friends (I am writing this in my office emotionally exhausted after officiating a funeral for a longtime church member).

Jesus saved me by atoning for *my* sins. I believe, with Martin Luther, that, "except thou be found in the number of those that say 'our sins,' that is, of those that have the doctrine of faith, and teach, hear, learn, love, and believe that same, there is no salvation for thee."[1] Faith is personal, and no amount of church attendance nor length of church membership will earn you a place in heaven. The church, in and of itself, saves no one. Only grace received through faith can do that: "If you confess with your mouth that Jesus is Lord and believe in your heart that God raised him from the dead, you will be saved" (Rom 10:9).

---

1. Luther, *Commentary on Galatians*, 4.

CHURCHING

The gospel can be separated from the church. One can imagine someone coming to faith in Jesus Christ, forgiven from his sin and reconciled into a relationship with the Father, and never once attending, let alone joining, a local church. Take for example a convert on the mission field or an inmate serving a life sentence (though some prisons do have churches). That person will join God's people in eternity. Next to Jesus on the cross, the dying thief rejoiced to see that fountain of grace in his day, apart from membership in a church. Those who have dechurched would argue that, since the gospel can be separated from the church, surely that makes the church unessential; what matters is a relationship between me and God, and we don't need institutional religion to get in between us. Maybe the church just isn't essential for every Christian?

Yet, such a reductionist view of Christianity does no one any good. It does no good to the church, which is reduced both in gifting and resources from the loss of a dechurched Christian. It does the dechurched Christian no good, as he or she loses a biblical means of grace towards maturity in the faith. It does the world no good, as the witness of the gospel is exponentially enhanced by Christian love displayed in the church. It does no good for the glory of God, as the church is established for the praise of his glorious grace: "And he put all things under his feet and gave him as head over all things to the church, which is his body, the fullness of him who fills all in all" (Eph 1:22–23).

If someone argues the church is unessential, the question should be, Unessential for what? If Christianity is reduced to "how we get to heaven," then maybe we could consider the church unessential. Even so, I am not sure. As bearer of the kingdom's "keys" (Matt 16:19), the church ensures spiritual authenticity as part of its role. But for the sake of argument, let us grant the point. The church is essential if Christianity is going to be more than a ticket to heaven. It is essential for Christian discipleship. It is essential for Christian witness. It is essential for the moral preservation of the world. It is essential for the glory of God. To say it is unessential is to reduce Christianity into what so many dechurched Christians

CONCLUSION

would despise most about institutional religion: an anemic faith beneficial for no one, save the individualistic preferences of its pontiff—namely, myself.

This is not a choice between the church *or* the gospel; it is a choice of the church *for* the gospel. It is far more likely we will lose the gospel with an unchurched Christianity than with a robust ecclesiology. In other words, church done right, engaging in all its God-granted responsibilities, protects gospel centrality from various pitfalls (a mere social gospel being one example and so-called easy-believism or cheap grace being another). A dechurched Christianity becomes even more subject to theological error or heresy, a faith shaped more by relativism than by the gospel. Is this not the direction dechurching has led us? "This is the real story of religion in America," writes Ross Douthat. "For all its piety and fervor, today's United States needs to be recognized for what it really is: not a Christian country, but a nation of heretics."[2] Biblical and orthodox Christianity is churching Christianity.

My desire to keep the gospel at the center of the Christian life leads me to promote churching even more. It is just such a high view of the church that is the best, albeit still imperfect, safeguard to persevere in gospel centrality. Those who love the gospel should love the church, just as those who love the church should love the gospel. It is time Christians regain the robust role of the church in the Christian life. Instead of a minimalistic view of Christianity, reducing the faith to its bare "essentials," let us embrace the full array of Christian ecclesiology. And let us do it for the sake of the gospel.

---

2. Douthat, *Bad Religion*, 6.

Bibliography

Augustine. "Letter 98 (A.D. 408)." Translated by J. G. Cunningham. From vol. 1 of *Nicene and Post-Nicene Fathers*, First Series. Edited by Philip Schaff. Buffalo, NY: Christian Literature, 1887. Revised by Kevin Knight. https://www.newadvent.org/fathers/1102098.htm.

Bainton, Roland. *Here I Stand: A Life of Martin Luther.* New York: Penguin, 1977.

Bauer, Walter, et al. *Greek-English Lexicon of the New Testament and Other Early Christian Literature.* 3rd ed. Chicago: University of Chicago Press, 2000.

Beckmann, Johann. *A History of Inventions, Discoveries, and Origins.* Translated by William Johnston. London: Henry G. Bohn, 1846.

Bonhoeffer, Dietrich. *Life Together: A Discussion of Christian Fellowship.* Translated by John W. Doberstein. New York: Harper Collins, 1954.

Broome, John David. *Life, Ministry, and Journals of Hezekiah Smith: Pastor of the First Baptist Church of Haverhill, Massachusetts, 1765 to 1805, and Chaplain in the American Revolution, 1775 to 1780.* Springfield, MI: Particular Baptist, 2004.

Connor, Philip. "6 Facts About South Korea's Growing Christian Population." Pew Research Center. Aug. 12, 2014. https://www.pewresearch.org/short-reads/2014/08/12/6-facts-about-christianity-in-south-korea/#:~:text=In%201900%2C%20only%201%25%20of,Korea%20over%20the%20past%20century.

Cyprian. "Treatise 1: On the Unity of the Church." Translated by Robert Ernest Wallis. From vol. 5 of *Ante-Nicene Fathers.* Edited by Alexander Roberts, et al. Buffalo, NY: Christian Literature, 1886. Revised by Kevin Knight. http://www.newadvent.org/fathers/050701.htm.

Davis, Jim, and Michael Graham. *The Great Dechurching: Who's Leaving, Why Are They Going, and What Will It Take to Bring Them Back?* Grand Rapids: Zondervan Reflective, 2023.

DeYoung, Kevin, and Greg Gilbert. *What Is the Mission of the Church? Making Sense of Social Justice, Shalom, and the Great Commission.* Wheaton, IL: Crossway, 2011.

BIBLIOGRAPHY

Douthat, Ross. *Bad Religion: How We Became a Nation of Heretics.* New York: Free, 2012.

Earls, Aaron. "Churchgoers May Be Overconfident in Old Testament Knowledge." Lifeway Research. Aug. 13, 2024. https://research.lifeway.com/2024/08/13/churchgoers-may-be-overconfident-in-old-testament-knowledge/.

Eusebius. *The History of the Church.* Translated by G. A. Williamson. Harmondsworth, UK: Penguin, 1984.

Fee, Gordon D. *The First Epistle to the Corinthians.* New International Commentary on the New Testament. Grand Rapids: Eerdmans, 1987.

Finke, Roger, and Rodney Stark. *The Churching of America, 1776–2005: Winners and Losers in our Religious Economy.* Newark, NJ: Rutgers University Press, 2005.

George, Christian. "6 Quotes Spurgeon Didn't Say." Spurgeon Center. Aug. 8, 2017. https://www.spurgeon.org/resource-library/blog-entries/6-quotes-spurgeon-didnt-say/.

Green, Michael. *Evangelism in the Early Church.* Grand Rapids: Eerdmans, 2003.

Guinness, Os. *Dining with the Devil: The Megachurch Movement Flirts with Modernity.* Grand Rapids: Baker, 1993.

Hansen, Collin, and Jonathan Leeman. *Rediscover Church: Why the Body of Christ Is Essential.* Wheaton, IL: Crossway, 2021.

Harnack, Adolf. *Mission and Expansion of the Early Christianity in the First Three Centuries.* Translated by James Moffatt. New York: Harper & Row, 1962.

Holiday, Ryan. *Perennial Seller: The Art of Making and Marketing Work That Lasts.* London: Profile, 2017.

Holland, Tom. *Dominion: How the Christian Revolution Remade the World.* New York: Basic, 2019.

Horton, Michael. *Ordinary: Sustainable Faith in a Radical, Restless World.* Grand Rapids: Zondervan, 2014.

Hunter, James Davison. *To Change the World: The Irony, Tragedy, and Possibility of Christianity in the Modern World.* Oxford: Oxford University Press, 2010.

Idleman, Kyle. *Not a Fan: Becoming a Completely Committed Follower of Jesus.* Grand Rapids: Zondervan, 2011.

Jackson, J. David. *New England Culture and Ministry Dynamics: Where You Serve Makes a Difference in How You Serve.* Simpsonville, SC: Screven and Allen, 2018.

Joshua Project. "What Is the 10/40 Window?" https://joshuaproject.net/resources/articles/10_40_window.

Julian the Apostate. "Letters (1923)." Translated by W. C. Wright. Early Church Fathers. https://www.tertullian.org/fathers/julian_apostate_letters_1_trans.htm.

Bibliography

Leeman, Jonathan. *Authority: How Godly Rule Protects the Vulnerable, Strengthens Communities, and Promotes Human Flourishing.* Wheaton, IL: Crossway, 2023.

Lewis, C. S. *The Complete C. S. Lewis Signature Classics.* New York: Harper Collins, 2002.

Ligonier. "The Sabbath." https://learn.ligonier.org/guides/the-sabbath.

Louw, Johannes P., and Eugene Albert Nida. *Greek-English Lexicon of the New Testament: Based on Semantic Domains.* New York: United Bible Societies, 1996.

Luther, Martin. *Commentary of Galatians.* Translated by Erasmus Middleton. Grand Rapids: Kregel, 1979.

Origen. "Contra Celsum, Book III." Translated by Frederick Crombie. From vol. 4 of *Ante-Nicene Fathers.* Edited by Alexander Roberts, et al. Buffalo, NY: Christian Literature, 1885. Revised by Kevin Knight. https://www.newadvent.org/fathers/04163.htm.

Packer, J. I. "What Is the Future of Evangelicalism?" *Modern Reformation*, Nov. 6, 2008. https://www.modernreformation.org/resources/articles/what-is-the-future-of-evangelicalism-8.

Page, Guy. "Number of Vermont Evangelicals Doubled in Last Decade." *Vermont Daily Chronicle*, Aug. 18, 2023. https://vermontdailychronicle.com/number-of-vermont-evangelicals-doubled-in-last-decade/.

Rainer, Thom S. "Lifeway Research: The Number 1 Reason for the Decline in Church Attendance . . ." Lifeway Research. Dec. 17, 2018. https://research.lifeway.com/2018/12/17/the-number-1-reason-for-the-decline-in-church-attendance/.

———. "The One Thing that Solves Most Church Problems (only 1% of Churches Actually Do This." *Church Answers* (blog), Nov. 1, 2023. https://churchanswers.com/blog/the-one-thing-that-solves-most-church-problems-only-1-of-church-actually-do-this/.

Roach, David. "To Grow in New England, Southern Baptists Crack 'Yankee Stoicism.'" *Christianity Today*, Oct. 6, 2023. https://www.christianitytoday.com/2023/10/southern-baptist-new-england-sbc-growth-church-planting-nam/.

Spurgeon, C. H. *The Metropolitan Tabernacle Pulpit Sermons.* 63 vols. London: Passmore & Alabaster, 1891.

Storms, Sam. *Practicing the Power: Welcoming the Gifts of the Holy Spirit in Your Life.* Grand Rapids: Zondervan, 2017.

Stott, John. *The Living Church: Convictions of a Lifelong Pastor.* Downers Grove, IL: InterVarsity, 2007.

Strong, Augustus Hopkins. *Systematic Theology.* 3 vols. Philadelphia: American Baptist Publication Society, 1907.

Torik, Aleksandr. *Churching for Beginners to Church Life.* Translated by Nathan K. Williams. Bellingham, WA: Logos Digital, 2011. E-book.

Trulson, Reid S. *Charlotte Atlee White Rowe: The Story of America's First Appointed Woman Missionary.* Macon, GA: Mercer University Press, 2021.

BIBLIOGRAPHY

US Department of State. "2020 Report on International Religious Freedom: North Korea." https://www.state.gov/wp-content/uploads/2021/05/240282-KOREA-DEM-REP-2020-INTERNATIONAL-RELIGIOUS-FREEDOM-REPORT.pdf.

———. "2022 Report on International Religious Freedom: Brazil." https://www.state.gov/wp-content/uploads/2023/05/441219-BRAZIL-2022-INTERNATIONAL-RELIGIOUS-FREEDOM-REPORT.pdf.

Whittock, Martyn, and Hannah Whittock. *The Vikings: From Odin to Christ.* Oxford: Lion Hudson, 2018.

Witmer, Stephen. *A Big Gospel in Small Places: Why Ministry in Forgotten Communities Matters.* Downers Grove, IL: InterVarsity, 2019.

www.ingramcontent.com/pod-product-compliance
Lightning Source LLC
Chambersburg PA
CBHW072159100426
42738CB00011BA/2473